The Caste and Class Controversy

Ravi Mehra, *Publisher*
Marie I. Corsalini, *Editor*
GENERAL HALL, INC.
Publishers
23-45 Corporal Kennedy St.
Bayside, New York 11360

The Caste and Class Controversy

Charles Vert Willie

Harvard University

GENERAL HALL, INC.
Publishers
23-45 Corporal Kennedy Street
Bayside, New York 11360

CASTE AND CLASS CONTROVERSY

ISBN: 0—930390—35—0 [paper]
        0—930390—36—9 [cloth]

Library of Congress Catalog Card
Number: 79—54687 Manufactured in the
United States of America

THIS BOOK IS DEDICATED
TO THE MEMORY OF
W.E.B. DuBois
AND
E. FRANKLIN FRAZIER
who identified Caste and Class
as the problems of the twentieth century

Contents

Summary And Conclusion

PREFACE

The summer of 1977 provided for me clear and present evidence that something is wrong with the way we analyze race relations in the United States. During the first week in September of that year William J. Wilson, a black professor of Sociology at the University of Chicago presented a lecture at the annual meeting of the prestigeous Sociological Research Association and told that group that social class has become more important than race in determining access to economic power and privileges for blacks in the United States. This conclusion later was included in his book on *The Declining Significance of Race* that was published in 1978. Further, he said that the rate of entry into positions of influence and prestige by blacks who are educated and have talent, in some instances, is greater than that for whites with similar qualifications.

Less than two weeks before Professor Wilson delivered his treatise on "The Declining Significance of Race," *The New York Times* (August 29, 1977, p. 35c) published the report of an interview with Sanford Allen, a black violinist with the New York Philharmonic, who announced his intention to resign from his position in that prestigious organization. He said he was "simply tired of being a symbol." At that time Allen was the only black who had been a member of that orchestra that was more than one and one-third centuries old. He charged the more influential and prestigious symphony orchestras of this nation, such as the Boston Symphony, the Chicago Symphony and two or three others, with running a closed shop that has

1

resulted in black exclusion. Allen said he often got telephone calls from good black musicians who had heard about a Philharmonic audition coming up. When they asked, "Is it really any point in coming," the black violinist said he was not always sure how to answer that question, since he then was the only black member of the orchestra that he joined in 1962; during a decade and a half, no other blacks had been hired. The Allen experience did not fit well with the Wilson pronouncement.

Finally, as the summer of 1977 drew near the end, a nation-wide Harris Survey revealed that 48 per cent of the blacks believed their progress had been "too slow" while 55 per cent of the whites thought that black people had tried to "move too fast" in achieving racial equality. Moreover, nearly three-fifths of the population believed that the black executive of the National Urban League was not justified in publicly criticizing the President of the United States for "neglecting blacks, the poor and other minorities," (*Boston Globe*, September 12, 1977).

Meanwhile, the Census Bureau reported that the number of blacks enrolled in college during the Bicentennial Year was 1.1 million, that this number represented more than a three-fold increase in one decade, and that about seven per cent of all blacks were college graduates, representing approximately a two-fold increase in one decade.

Also during the summer of 1977, arguments -- pro and con -- raged over radio, television, and in magazines and newspapers concerning whether these educated blacks could continue their education in graduate professional schools such as medical schools. The issue was whether spaces could be reserved in entering classes for minorities who might not otherwise be admitted because of the effects of previous discrimination. Some claimed that quotas for blacks were unfair to whites. Others said, this was the only method that was just for all.

These many different issues, contrasting views, and contradictory themes that issued forth during the summer of 1977 indicated that if race was declining in significance for some people, it was increasing in significance for others. A problem with our analysis of race relations is that the focus usually is too narrow.

Any analysis of black gains or losses must also determine the significance of these for whites and vice versa. A comparative or comprehensive analysis that focuses on all is necessary because the majority and minority are linked together in the United States in a symbiotic relationship metaphorically labeled by Anthropologist Stanley Diamond as "a hellish minuet" (Diamond, *Dissent,* Autumn 1965, p. 474). I arrived at a similar conclusion after studying the case histories of 12 black middle-class, working-class and lower-class families. On the basis of that analysis, I concluded "[1] that black and white families in America share a common core of values, [2] that they adapt to the society and its values in different ways, largely because of racial discrimination, and [3] that the unique adaptation of blacks is further differentiated by variations in style of life by social class. Any assumption that the life of blacks in America can be understood independent of their involvement with whites appears to be unwarranted" (Willie, *A New Look at Black Families,* 1976, p. 195).

Blacks have seen their population differentiate in a short period of time from a more or less homogeneous category of poor people of whom less than one-eighth was middle class as late as the mid-20th century, according to E. Franklin Frazier (Frazier, *The Negro Family in Chicago*), to the last quarter of this 100-year span in which about one-third of the black population is middle class or higher.

If one were to analyze black gains from an affirmative action perspective and interpret them as white losses, then Wilson could have used the same set of data but carried the title "The Increasing Significance of Race for Whites." Indeed whites have seen their authority and power eroded over the years from the age of slavery when blacks were totally under their control and were of little, if any, competition to the present time when courts of law are rendering decisions in favor of black plaintiffs and against white defendants and are requiring remedies to redress past grievances and the payment of penalties for damages that resulted from deliberate efforts on the part of whites to harm blacks. For whites who must adapt to and abide by court orders that favor blacks, race clearly is a salient feature that encroaches upon their previous way of life.

The turbulence in community life today because of court-ordered school desegregation and the dither of some whites about affirmative action goals, practices and procedures indicate that race is very much salient for whites and appears to be increasing rather than decreasing in significance. The national interest generated by the Bakke Case that alleged "reverse discrimination" is indicative of the saliency of race to many whites.

W. E. B. DuBois said that the problem of the twentieth century would be that of color, and E. Franklin Frazier said that social stratification is the most significant frame of reference for studying social change in community life. Together, these two social scientists identified the issues of this age that are shaking the foundation of this nation -- race and social class.

Wherever these two parameters are found, there is the tension of inequality. When ever these two parameters intersect, there is a compounded tension of inequality; together, caste and class are explosive. William Wilson's book on *The Declining Significance of Race* focused on the agony that racial and socio-economic inequality have generated in a society where justice is significant, and contributed to a minor explosion.

The analysis in this book demonstrates why many have been swift to reject the Wilson hypothesis that social class is a more significant determinant of life-chances than race in the United States at this period in its history. At stake is the continued implementation of affirmative action plans and antidiscrimination programs.

Part I of this book lays out alternative interpretations and comes to the conclusion that institutional oppression due to elitism as well as racism is alive and well in America. This conclusion is based on a Review of Research in which the author has been engaged for more than a quarter of a century. Also, Part I presents a theoretical discussion of class, status, and race in the system of social stratification in the United States. It presents the author's own understanding of these concepts based on a variety of experiences in research and policy matters and includes some of the material used in his debate with Wilson at Michigan State University in November of 1978 and at the Eastern Sociological Society in March, 1979.

Part II consists of Analytical Comments by other social scientists. Three book reviews, original essays and an excerpt from a National Urban League report are included.

The Summary and Conclusion consists of commentaries prepared by the author and William J. Wilson for the 1978 July/August issue of *Society* magazine, and the Statement issued by the Association of Black Sociologists. Appreciation is expressed to *Contemporary Sociology, Social Forces, Change* magazine, *Society*, the Research Division of the National Urban League, and *The Washington Post* for permission to reprint material that they had published.

If controversy is the creative kernel of history and truth has a better chance of emerging from controversy, this book is offered as a contribution to that truth which is always partial until confronted by another version.

C. V. W.
August, 1979
Cambridge, Massachusetts

1

SIGNIFICANCE OF THE DEBATE ON CASTE AND CLASS

In 1978 the University of Chicago Press published a small volume, less than 200 pages of text, that has stimulated a large controversy. *The Declining Significance of Race* was the title of the book and William Julius Wilson, Professor of Sociology at the University, was its author.

Wilson presented an elaborate discussion on variations in the system of production in the United States and its relationship to black-white contacts. Stage one, according to Wilson, was antebellum slavery, "the period of plantation economy and racial-caste oppression." The last quarter of the nineteenth century to the New Deal was stage two, the period of industrial expansion. The third stage began in the post-World War II era, crystalizing during the 1960s and 1970s. Wilson said this stage "may be characterized as the period of progressive transition from racial inequalities to class inequalities" (Wilson, 1978: 2-3). The analysis of the nature of race relations and the ways that black-white contacts are influenced by the prevailing means of production, Wilson claims, is the "central argument" of the book (Wilson, 1978:3). If this indeed had been the central theme of the book few would have taken note of it.

Wilson had more to say; and what he argued had serious implications for affirmative action programs for racial minorities. Wilson claimed that "the black middle class is enjoying unprecedented success in finding white collar jobs" (Wilson, 1978:99), that "equal employment legislation in the early sixties have virtually eliminated the tendency of employers to create a split labor market in which black labor is deemed cheaper than white labor regardless of the work performed" (Wilson, 1978:110), that "economic class is now a more important factor than race in determining job placement for blacks" (Wilson, 1978:120), and that poverty among inner-city blacks is largely a function of their relatively poor training and inferior schooling (Wilson, 1978:121).

Meanwhile, Wilson sprinkled his argument about the economic determination of race relations with a few anti-black themes such as this one: "The significance of black political control of the central city is not that it will provide a basis for economic and social mobility in the black community...but that it will heighten the racial antagonism that occasionally surfaces over issues such as school busing and residential segregation" (Wilson, 1978, 120). Wilson's analysis fits into the age-old practice of blaming the victim. Here, he suggests that racial antagonism may be directly linked with the increasing capacity of blacks to control politically their own destiny in the urban environment.

The serious problem about Wilson's book is that it is part of a series of publications dating back to *Inequality* by Christopher Jencks, and *The Negro Family: A Case for National Action* by Daniel P. Moynihan that cast doubt on the focus of the freedom movement among minorities. *The Negro Family* prepared by the United States Labor Department and also called the Moynihan Report, suggested that poverty might be perpetuated among black people in the United States.

largely because of their alleged unstable family structures (U.S. Labor Department, 1965). Moynihan, of
course, did not rule out increasing the economic
resources of the black family as a way of contributing
to its viability; but it is clear that the social integration
of family members should receive priority attention,
according to his analysis. Many black ghetto dwellers
and some social scientists disagreed with this assertion
and assessment. The reason for the continuing poverty
and unequal opportunity of black people in America,
they said, was a blocked opportunity system, blocked
largely because of racial discrimination.

Leaders in the black community warned that if
conclusions about the black family in the Moynihan
Report were used as a basis for national policy, the
freedom movement would suffer a major setback as
reform efforts would be refocused on changing individuals and families rather than changing institutions and systems (Willie, 1970:2). In other words, acceptance of the Moynihan Report and its analysis
would identify the victim and his or her family structure as the major contribution to their disadvantaged
circumstnces rather than the system and its various
forms of institutional oppression

Moynihan contended that he prepared the report
on The Negro Family as a way of helping poor people, as evidence that the federal government should
provide a family allowance (Willie, 1969:126). His
claim and that of Wilson are similar. Wilson said that
his book was for the purpose of helping poor people, of
alerting the society to "the consequences of ignoring
these structural dimensions in explaining inequality, as
far as the black poor are concerned." Indeed, he stated
that "even if all racial discrimination were eliminated
today, the situation of poor blacks will not be substantially improved unless something is done to remove the
structural barriers to decent jobs created by changes in
our system of production" (Wilson, 1978:19). That

racial discrimination should be discounted as being less significant in affecting the life-chances of blacks than their family composition, on the one hand, or their economic status, on the other, is not demonstrated either by Moynihan or by Wilson.

If the Moynihan Report had not been effectively challenged it would have become the policy statement that served as the basis of the 1966 White House Conference on Civil Rights; for the President's Howard University speech in 1965 that a White House Conference would be called the next year to discover ways to help American black people move beyond opportunity to achievement sounded similar to many of the ideas advocated by Daniel Patrick Moynihan.

The prize-winning book *Inequality* by Christopher Jencks and associates was the next publication that is similar to that of William Wilson. It, too, had to be challenged to prevent permanent harm of public policy based on its conclusion. Howard Taylor said that "Jencks...takes considerable liberties in discussing the effects of integration, segregation, race, etc., upon occupational and income inequality. He clearly infers that education is not related to success for black people; that if blacks want more money, then more education will not get it." Then Taylor introduced a surprising piece of evidence against Jencks. He said that inferences by Jencks were based on a statistical technique called path analysis and that the data used in the Jencks study was obtained from "native white nonfarm males who took an armed forces IQ test!" In fact, Taylor said, "Not one single path analysis in the entire report is performed on even one black sample" (Taylor, 1973:245-246). Thus, the ideas discussed in *Inequality* are inappropriate as the basis of public policy so far as blacks are concerned.

Jencks committed the error of projecting his findings about inequality upon blacks without including them in his study. Wilson committed the reverse of this same error. His study is of the relative effects of race and social class on life-chances; yet the data he analyzed were limited largely to the black population. "To interpret and explain the basis of racial change in America from a macrosociological perspective" (Wilson, 1978:2), which is the task that Wilson assigned himself, a comparative analysis of the life-chances of racial minorities and the racial majority is essential. Wilson mentioned whites from time to time and included in his book a few tables that consisted of data on blacks and whites. But there was not a systematic comparative study of both racial populations.

Beyond Jencks' error of projecting, Harold Howe II, former Commissioner of Education of the United States, said that "Jencks' view that luck and personality factors were more important than education in producing differentials in income was rapidly parlayed in popular articles and editorials across the United States into arguments that schools didn't matter and that money spent on schools was wasted." The initial results of Jencks' work, according to Howe, "was to hurt children." He said that "the counter-fire from knowledgeable critics...did not appear in time to get the public notice to undo the harm" (Howe, 1976).

The same can be said of Wilson's work. The *Washington Post* called the lineup for and against the Wilson thesis that economic class is more important than race in predetermining job placement and occupational mobility, "an unprecedented standoff among black intellectuals" (West, 1979:C13). A resolution adopted by the Association of Black Sociologists expressed concern that the book "was considered sufficiently factual to merit the Spivack award from the American Sociological Association." The resolution reminded the public that "In the past reactionary groups have seized upon inappropriate analyses as a basis for the further suppression of blacks." And the black sociologists said that they were disturbed over the policy implications that may derive from Wilson's work (Association of Black Sociologists, 1978).

The harm that the Association of Black Sociologists predicted began to surface soon after the publication of the Wilson book. Public opinion molders such as Albert Shanker, President of the United Federation of Teachers, wrote that "things have changed, progress has been made" by blacks. He embraced the opinions of two Fordham University researchers (Louis Henri Bolce III and Susan H. Gray) who asserted that activist social scientists have down-played the progress deliberately "in the hope that by maintaining a picture of blacks as poor, uneducated, unskilled -- and on the verge of rioting because of these conditions -- the public and government would be motivated to improve race relations by doing more for minorities" (Shanker, 1979:E9). Shanker implied that special efforts no longer were necessary because of the progress that minorities had made. He cited the fact that today 70 percent of black families are above the poverty level. Shanker, like Wilson, did not present a comparative picture of affluence. He did not mention that 90 percent of white families are above the poverty level.

An editor who is white and the publisher of an important social science magazine described the Wilson book as "important and provocative" and the statement by the Association of Black Sociologists as "intemperate" with "no other purpose than frustrating discussion rather than stimulating new directions for research in the area of black life in America." This editor's remarks were similar to those of the Fordham University researchers that were reported by Shanker.

Not all whites held similar views on the issue, however. A white member of the American Sociological Association who specialized in race relations research said, "It is indeed sad that Wilson's book has become sociologists' and society's pacifier in this period of serious retrogression."

While the issue has been misidentified in the press as a squabble between blacks, the *Washington Post* alluded to a deeper meaning of the controversy when reporter Hollie West stated that some who oppose Wilson "fear that the idea's acceptance could wipe out affirmative action and anti-discrimination programs" (West, 1979:C1). The member of the American Sociological Association mentioned earlier said that "American racism today touches even the most elite, moneyed, famous, and talented American blacks, as well as those who could be great but never got a chance." Allan Bakke demonstrated that whites have a stake in whether the public and government are motivated to do more for minorities.

If the Wilson work becomes the basis for doing less to overcome the inequities between the races such as, for example, cutting back efforts to eliminate the disproportionate number of blacks below the poverty line, then it indeed should be classified as a harmful document.

One significance of Wilson's book, according to Nathan Glazer, is that "It is the first time a black social scientists has said [these things] with such strength" (West, 1979). If Wilson's analysis is a "misrepresentation of the black experience" as claimed by the Association of Black Sociologists, then one can understand how the race of the author is an additional factor that has contributed to the controversy. Actually, the controversy is of significance for the total society. As stated by John Kennedy, "The rights of [all] are diminished when the rights of one...are threatened" (Willie, 1978:60).

Several years ago, E. Franklin Frazier said that "the social stratification of community...[is]...the most important frame of reference for studying...social changes in the life of...any urbanized group" (Frazier, 1968:141). Earlier, W. E. B. DuBois said that race would be the salient issue of the 20th century. The debate that the Wilson work has stimulated then, goes to the heart of the American experience -- its system of social stratification, esteem, and power: who shall be on top and who shall be on bottom? One could call Wilson's book a treatist on status politics that, in the end, is an apology for the dominant people of power despite his protestations that he is concerned about helping poor people. I make this statement because of the findings of Robert Hauser and David Featherman that "racial discrimination in the process of stratification is primarily socioeconomic" (Hauser and Featherman, 1977:xxv). Wilson ducks the issue of whether or not socioeconomic status in the United States is a dependent variable -- dependent, in part, on race. He prefers to identify social class as a variable that is dependent, in part, on education. He said that "access to the means of production is increasingly based on education." Then he implied that the position of "the black underclass" is solidified in the "low-wage sector" not so much because of their low racial estate due to discrimination but because of their inferior education (Wilson, 1978:151). Both the Hauser and Featherman statement mentioned above and the conclusion of James B. Conant differ with Wilson.

Conant claimed that "a caste system finds its clearest manifestation in an educational system" (Conant, 1961:11), and that "Racial discrimination makes unemployment chronic for the Negro male, North and South" (Conant, 1961:37). This is another way of stating that "racial discrimination...is primarily socioeconomic" and that whites are the beneficiaries and blacks are the victims of such discrimination. Wilson alluded to this fact but did not examine it in detail when he said, "Increasingly, Jewish leaders are talking about the threat that black advancement poses to Jews" (Wilson, 1978:119).

The fact is that equality of access and an equitable

participation in the economy and social system by blacks, browns, and whites threatens none and enhances all. As stated by Conant, "a healthy society requires a sound economy and high employment" (Conant, 1961:34). The under- or over-representation of any group in any sector is an imbalance and a potential threat to all if not handled in a way that is fair. John Rawls has reminded us that no one should gain or lose from one's initial position in society "without giving or receiving compensating advantages in return" (Rawls, 1971:101).

If unemployed, out-of-school young blacks in the inner-city are "social dynamite" as labeled by Conant (Conant, 1961:146), if "access to the means of production is increasingly based on educational criteria" as claimed by Wilson (Wilson, 1978:151), then we ought to invest "more than proportionately in the children of the poor...[so that]...high quality schools...[may]... compensate for the very low investment which [poor] families are able to make in their offspring..." as called for by John Kenneth Galbraith (Galbraith, 1958:256-258). Such would be an appropriate way of giving to the disadvantaged compensating advantages mentioned by Rawls.

One way to insure that poor, unemployed, inner-city blacks are not discriminated against and are given compensating advantages is for blacks to participate in the decision-making structures of urban communities. Wilson questions the value of this approach and asserts that "the fundamental bases of the urban crisis are not amenable to urban political solutions" (Wilson, 1978:140). The appropriation of public funds to support public education is a local political decision. If education is directly related to the inability of inner-city blacks to participate effectively in the labor force, then a political solution to this problem is to upgrade inner-city schools by allocating more money for them. Because Wilson casts doubt on this and other **political** solutions (despite the fact that more money for slum schools was recommended by a former Harvard president and a well-known Harvard economist approximately two decades ago), his analysis must be classified as *the grand apology* for the status quo.

The social dynamite in our inner-city urban metropolitan areas exploded in the 1960s and could explode again during the 1980s if effective action is not taken to ameliorate the circumstances and conditions of the poor. Thus, Wilson's analysis -- though faulty --has been of benefit in stimulating a national debate on the relative contribution of caste and class to individual and group life-chances.

One reason why blacks such as Kenneth B. Clark, the Association of Black Sociologists, and others have joined the debate and have vehemently denounced the Wilson hypothesis is that it offends their common sense. Several black social scientists and members of the families with whom they are affiliated have been victims of racial oppression at all levels of the social stratification hierarchy in the past and in the present. Moreover, the Wilson hypothesis that *"economic class is now a more important factor than race in determining job placement for blacks"* (Wilson, 1978:120) is contrary to what sensible people commonly read in the daily newspaper.

The American Telephone and Telegraph Company, according to *The Washington Post*, is an example of an American industry that refused to hire, train, and promote blacks, other minorities and women in an equitable way until it was hauled into court. The consent decree required AT and T "to use goals, timetables an other prodding devices short of fixed quotas to end discrimination..." (Dewar, 1978:A1). Contrary to Wilson's claim, blacks and other minorities had not received unprecendented opportunities at the managerial level in that industry. The consent decree was signed in 1973. It took AT and T five years to come within 99 percent of its affirmative action target. In terms of overall employment, minorities accounted for 16.6 percent of all workers in 1978 (the year that the Supreme Court affirmed the legality of the plan). This proportion was up from 13.8 percent five years earlier. The five-year period after the plan was ordered, the proportion of minorities in management at AT and T doubled from 4.6 percent to 8.7 percent (Dewar, 1978:A7). The AT and T experience, as reported in the newspaper, clearly indicated that blacks and other racial minorities were not receiving a disproportionate share of high-paying jobs compared with whites and that affirmative action law had not eliminated a split labor market in terms of wages paid in one of America's largest industries until it was hauled into court and compelled to pay equitably and to cease discriminating. The court found that the "particular pattern of discrimination" at AT and T had "detrimental effects" and required a specific plan to counteract them. According to the *Afro-American* newspaper, AT and T "is expected to eventually pay $100 million in compensation to women and minorities" as a penalty for past acts of discrimination (Crane, 1979:3).

It is appropriate that this debate on the relative contribution of race and socioeconomic status to life-chances be joined by whites as well as blacks as a way of clarifying the contribution of social class and social caste to inequality and oppression. Poor whites over the years have suffered the institutional oppression of social class without recognizing the function of the class system and how it has contributed to their difficulties. In some instances, poor whites have been liberated from the yoke of class oppresssion by the resistance and freedom movements mounted by racial minorities to overcome the institutional oppression of caste and class.

A lack of understanding of institutional oppression in recent years was manifested by a predominantly white group of workers, the Communication Workers of America and the Telephone Coordinating Council of the International Brotherhood of Electrical Workers. These unions sued to block the implementation of the affirmative action plan of AT and T, claiming not only that it used an illegal device to remedy the effects of past discrimination but also that it was improper. It is difficult to comprehend how a predominantly white labor union of men and women workers could classify as improper a plan that would lead to the hiring, training, and promotion of "tens of thousands" of white women as well as blacks and other minorities (Dewar, 1978:A1). The presence of a social caste system in the United States has distracted lesser affluent whites from understanding some of the oppressive effects of a social class system. The actions of the unions reflect this misunderstanding.

An experience from the past further demonstrates the ignorance of some whites of the institutional oppression of a social class system. Moreover, it is an example of how liberation for whites from the effects of social class has been a byproduct of the rebellion of blacks against the oppression of social caste and social class. W. E. B. DuBois stated that "the public school systems, in most Southern states, began with the enfranchisement of the Negro." Florida, for example, tried in 1850 to obtain schools for whites but was unsuccessful. DuBois said that educational historians agree that "under Negro suffrage came the law in 1869" that was "the real beginning" of the public school system in Florida. The same can be said of South Carolina, Georgia, Alabama, and Mississippi. Before the Civil War, DuBois said "the white laborers did not demand education....They accepted without murmur their subordination....Education they regarded as a luxury connected with wealth." DuBois claimed that it was the black folk in the South "who connected knowledge with power, who believed that education was the stepping-stone to wealth and respect, and [who believed] that wealth, without education, was crippled." Because of their belief, southern blacks during the period of Reconstruction demanded that public schools be established on a permanent basis "for all people and all classes" and they took affirmative action to implement these demands as lawmakers in state legislatures (DuBois, 1969:637-669).

The court-ordered AT and T plan to overcome discrimination in hiring, training, and promotion in industry and the governmental action by Reconstruction — state legislatures to establish public schools in the South are examples from the recent and remote past that whites have benefited from the resistance to institutional oppression by blacks and other racial minorities. This is further evidence that the debate on the relative effect of race and social class on life-chances is of importance to whites. Although the debate has surfaced among blacks, the outcome and the understandings derived from it could have serious consequences for all.

Indeed, the effects of social-class oppression may be more potent for poor whites at this period in American history since they have overcome the limitations of social caste. Social-class oppression is present for blacks too; but they may be unable to give their full attention to resisting it until they have effectively eliminated the oppression of social caste. Thus, Wilson's argument about the significance of social class with respect to life-chances may have greater applicability in terms of remedial action for whites than blacks at this period in American history. It would have been to the credit of Wilson had he alerted poor whites to the institutional oppression of social class as their priority target of resistance now and alerted all blacks to the institutional oppression of social caste and social class as their priority targets of resistance. Unfor-

tunately, Wilson did not do this. What he did was to
confuse the issue (1) by projecting the priority for poor
whites -- the resistance of social class oppression -- upon
blacks, and (2) by denying that the resistance of social
caste oppression is a necessary priority for blacks,
including the affluent.

Blacks in the United States experience a compounded situation of caste and class oppression. There
is interaction betweeen these two parameters. What
Wilson seemed to misunderstand is that a change in
one does not necessarily lead to a change in the other.
To be sure, there is increasing class differentiation
within the black population as there has been class differentiation for centuries within the white population.
But there also is caste differentiation between the
racial majority and racial minority populations today
as in centuries past. Moreover, an increase in the differentiation of one sector of the population by social
class does not necessarily result in a decrease in differentiation within the total population by social caste.
This is a principle that Wilson apparently missed in his
analysis.

At the beginning of this century, Booker T.
Washington and W. E. B. DuBois debated each other
on the relative benefits of career and classical education. That debate is not unlike the one between
William Wilson and other blacks that has erupted in
the final quarter of this century. Unfortunately, the
nation did not recognize that the outcome of the
Washington-DuBois debate was significant for the entire nation, did not make appropriate adjustments in
the system of higher education in accordance with their
conclusions, and therefore experienced an explosion on
college campuses across the nation that might have
been prevented if the wisdom the the Washington-
DuBois debate had been acknowledged and acted
upon affirmatively. That debate was ignored by the
majority as of little consequence, as merely an argu-

ment between two members of the minority. The
negative consequences of ignoring the signs of the time
for the nation as they have been pointed out by the insightful analyses of members of the minority are legion.
At a period in the American experience when elitism is
increasingly justified, when its excluding effects
negatively impact upon many of our citizens -- black,
brown, and white, denying them equal access to an
equitable participation in several institutions of our nation, a debate on the relative contribution of caste and
class to individual and group life-chances is relevant
for all. If such a debate is ignored as merely that of the
blacks again fussing with each other, we shall ignore it
at our peril as revealed by the history of this nation.

REFERENCES TO CHAPTER 1

Association of Black Sociologists, "Statement of the Association of Black Sociologists," September 6, 1978
Conant, James Bryant, *Slums and Suburbs,* New York: McGraw-Hill, 1961
Crane, Gordon W., "Sears Sues to Duck $100 Million Bias Penalty," *Afro-American, Week of January 30-February 3, 1979*
Dewar, Helen, *"Affirmative Action Plan at AT&T Is Permitted,"* The Washington Post, July 4, 1978, A1, A7
DuBois, W.E.B., *Black Reconstruction in America, 1860-1880,* New York: Atheneum (first published in 1935), 1969
Frazier, E. Franklin, "The Negro Family in Chicago" in G. Franklin Edwards (ed.), *Franklin Frazier on Race Relations,* Chicago: University of Chicago Press, 1968
Galbraith, John Kenneth, *The Affluent Society,* New York: Mentor Books, 1958
Hauser, Robert M. and Featherman, David L., *The Process of Stratification,* New York: Academic Press, 1977
Howe II, Harold, "Educational Research -- The Promise and the Problem." Address presented at the Annual Meeting of the American Educational Research Association, San Francisco, April 21, 1976
Shanker, Albert, "Black Community Holds Range of Views," *New York Times, February 4, 1979*
Taylor, Howard F., *"Playing the Dozens with Path Analysis"* in Raymond L. Hall (ed.), *Black Separatism and Social Reality,* New York: Pergamon, 1977
U.S. Labor Department, *The Negro Family: A Case for National Action,* Washington, D.C.: U.S. Government Printing Office, 1965
West, Hollie I., "Getting Ahead, and the Man Behind the Class-Race Furor," *Washington Post,* January 1, 1979, pp. C1, C13
Willie, Charles V., *Church Action in the World,* New York: Morehouse-Barlow, 1969
Willie, Charles V., *The Family Life of Black People,* Columbus, Ohio: Charles E. Merrill, 1970
Wilson, William J., "The Declining Significance of Race, Revisited but Not Revised," *Society,* 15, July/August 1978

A REVIEW OF RESEARCH

2

CLASS, STATUS AND RACE:
A Theoretical and Methodological Review

In all known human societies there is differentiation -- differentiation in the structural organization of a society and in the functional relationships of members to each other. Persons occupy different positional arrangements within a social organization and are accorded different rights, responsibilities, privileges, and prestige. As to function, different persons are expected to do different things to, for, or with specific individuals in a society. Loomis, Beegle and Longmore summarized these principles well in their monograph on class and social stratification: "Regardless of how much people in a given society are proclaimed to be equal, careful study will always reveal differences in rights, authority, privileges, responsibilities and prestige."[1]

Accepting this principle of human social organization, the research sociologist is faced then with the problem of identifying, measuring, and understanding patterns and modes of differentiation in the community. Anthropological data indicate that persons in different positions in human communities are accorded different honor, rank, and prestige. Studies also reveal that criteria for honor and rank vary from community to community; therefore, an understanding of prevailing values within a community must be had before one may select the more significant systems of differentiation for study. Since it is true that "most...human societies elaborate the process of ranking further by arranging certain social positions in a graded hierarchy of socially superior or inferior ranks,"[2] we may extend our studies of differentiation to considerations of social stratification which is a specific kind of social differentiation.

Kaufman states that "societies vary as to the dominant values on which the stratification is based. In present day America, for example, economic values have high priority whereas in medieval Europe the religious institution had relatively great importance."[3] Because successful activity in the economic system is valued in the society of the United States, many investigators have found the analysis of human differentiation associated with economic organization to be a fruitful area of research; this interest has given rise to several studies which investigated the system of stratification in American society in relation to one's position in the economic organization. More recently, however, investigators have indicated that they are concerned with patterns of social and economic or socio-economic stratification since, as stated by North and Hatt, "a man's job... is more than just a means of livelihood or an outlet for his creative energy; it is a vital influence on his existence even beyond working hours."[4]

The concept, "socio-economic status," which was introduced into the literature of social science in 1925 by Chapman and Sims in their journal article entitled "The Quantitative Measurement of Certain Aspects of Socio-Economic Status,"[5] was favorably accepted and quickly added to the professional jargon because it also focused on the social dimension of economic activity. To denote and measure socio-economic phenomena are still major methodological problems, however.

Among social scientists, unanimity does not exist on which variable, factors, or characters of the environment, population, and the behavior of people are the better indicators or reflectors of socio-economic stratification. When reference is made to socio-economic status, generally, it is believed that an individual or family of individuals is identified by standards associated with such factors as income, occupation, education, and material possessions.

There are a number of unanswered questions about the denotation of socio-economic status. Many of these questions must await the accumulation of more systematically gathered evidence before clarification is possible. One major theoretical problem is: should individuals with common attributes and ways of behaving (who may or may not be like-minded) be categorized as of the same class and stratum, or should like-minded individuals (who may or may not exhibit common attributes and ways of behaving) be categorized as of the same class and stratum? In many studies the first proposition is subscribed to either because it is assumed that, in most instances, persons with similar attributes will experience similar life-chances, or because information regarding how people feel about their positions in society is not available. While inadequate or unavailable data are realities which condition that which is studied and how it may be studied, one ought to decide which of the above propositions he or she subscribes to before proceeding with any study of socio-economic stratification if findings and interpretation of findings are to be clear and understandable.

No matter how one disposes of the issue mentioned above, the operational problem of denoting socio-economic status remains. From amongst the things that people are, do, or symbolize, what are the best indicators of socio-economic status? Shall it be education, occupation, income, material possession -- one,

some, or all of these, or even still some other indicators? Implicit in the preceding statement is another
question: Is there a single, or are there multiple orders
of socio-economic stratification within a community? If
there are multiple orders -- for example, education, occupation and income -- is each order of equal importance in indicating a person's socio-economic status
position? If multiple orders of status exist, do they converge into a single system of socio-economic stratification? If so, how do they converge? And finally, what
happens when, in time, one of the orders within the
composite stratification system changes in relation to
another status order? For example, what effect does a
change such as an increase in income for manual
workers and a relative decrease in income for white-
collar workers have upon the socio-economic status
positions of persons in these two occupation categories
when both income and occupation may be relevant to
defining one's position within the stratification hierarchy of a selected community?.

A dearth of theory underlies most of the studies of
socio-economic stratification, because many of the important theoretical questions have yet to be answered.
Before we get to the knotty problem of how the orders
of status may converge into a single system of socio-
economic stratification, there is the initial question of
what orders should be included in one's study when the
research is designed to delineate, for example, residential areas of varying socio-economic status. This problem was faced by three outstanding pioneers in their
ecological studies of total communities. The studies of
Chicago by Ernest Burgess,[6] New Haven by Maurice
Davie,[7] and 142 American cities by Homer Hoyt,[8] early
community studies in American sociology, offer a good
example of the interplay between theory and empiricism in the development of the field of social
stratification.

Pioneers among sociologists in the ecological study

of community organization were Ernest Burgess and
Robert Park at the University of Chicago, who, in the
1920 decade, supervised much ecological research on
Chicago. The famous concentric circle hypothesis
about urban growth emerged from these studies and
was set forth by Burgess in 1925. The five circular
zones which Burgess identified in Chicago were Zone I,
the central business distict; Zone II, an area in transition from residential to commercial usage surrounding
the downtown district; Zone III, the area of working
men's homes and persons who have escaped from the
slums; Zone IV, the residential area of high-class
apartments and exclusive single-family dwellings; Zone
V, the elite suburban area where commuters live.[9]

The Burgess, Davie, and Hoyt studies deserve
special mention because they represent major steps in
the evolution of social ecology as a method of investiga-
tion. In the 1920's and earlier when University of
Chicago sociologists began their studies, sociological
theory regarding the residential organization of urban
areas was minimal. Quickly during this decade movement from mere empiricism to theoretical considerations is seen. Contributing to the growth of ecological
theory were the Burgess concentric circle hypothesis
published in 1925, the refutation of this hypothesis by
Davie in 1937, and a further refutation of the Burgess
theory by Hoyt who also advanced his sector theory in
1939.

It was during the two decades between 1920 and
1940 that theory began to emerge pertaining to the importance of certain characteristics in differentiating
the city into relatively homogeneous residential
neighborhoods by socio-economic status. If not theory
regarding what ought to be included in an ecological
study of neighborhood differentiation, there certainly
was emerging theory regarding characteristics considered to be useless. For example, Burgess listed some
thirty or more characteristics in his study of Chicago

published in 1925. Leiffer included approximately
twenty characteristics in his study of Evanston in
1932.[10] In that same year, Green delineated cultural
areas in Cleveland using thirteen variables.[11] And
Davie reduced the number of variables to ten in his
study of New Haven published in 1937. Finally, Hoyt
in 1939 published his findings about the organization
of American cities based on an analysis in which only
eight factors were used to delineate neighborhoods.
Hence, the number of variables employed to delineate
ecological areas in urban communities is seen to
diminish from more than thirty in 1925 to eight in
1939. The use of fewer characteristics made possible
the comparison of neighborhood organization in one
city with that in another; this trend began with Davie
and his analysis of twenty cities reported in 1937 and
was further elaborated by Hoyt in his 1939 publication
which involved data obtained in 142 American cities.
Although the trend has been to reduce the variables
under study to a manageable number, there still is lack
of unanimity on exactly which variables are most
useful. As late as 1947 Stuart Queen stated that few investigators of the ecological distribution of mental
diseases in urban areas use the same socio-economic index.[12]

Upon two or three characteristics, however, some
agreement appears to have emerged during these early
decades in the study of urban communities. Between
1920 and 1940, there was fairly widespread belief that
rental, home value, and land value were useful indicators in differentiating city neighborhoods of varying socio-economic status. During these decades of early development, most ecological studies tended to be
descriptive only. Almost all of the studies used the base
map. Plotting the distribution of various demographic
characteristics on a city map was the principal technique of analysis. This procedure enabled the investigator to visualize those neighborhoods in which

certain characteristics tended to concentrate.

The descriptive studies of the past were not without value. Representations on social base maps indicated that persons with similar achieved attributes tended to live in similar sections of the city. Which attributes were more significantly associated with one's ecological area of residence and presumably one's position in the social stratification system were suggested but not determined in the pre-nineteen-forty analyses.

Further insights into the nature of socio-economic stratification and the organization and integration pattern of its major components have resulted from total community studies which utilized the methods of cultural anthropology. The studies of W. Lloyd Warner[13], [14] and A. B. Hollingshead [15], [16] are perhaps the best examples of how data from this kind of research have contributed to clarification of the theory of socio-economic stratification. Moving beyond purely descriptive activity, Warner and Hollingshead attempted to develop instruments of prediction.

Warner and his associates began with the following assumptions about social organization: (1) interacting persons in the social system of a community evaluate the participation of each other; (2) what an individual does, how and where he does it, is evaluated by those around him; (3) because of implicit or explicit awareness of patterns of ranking, community members translate their evaluations of an individual's participation into social class ratings.[17] These assumptions are based upon observations in many field studies in which Warner participated, such community studies as those of Yankee City, Old City, and Jonesville. These assumptions about American community life led Warner and associates to develop what is called the *evaluated participation method* for studying social stratification. Essentially, six steps are involved in getting an individual's social status rating by the evaluated participation method: ratings by mutual agreement, status reputation, symbolic placement, comparison, simple assignment to class and by institutional memberhsip.[18]

Warner states that the evaluated participation method is "a way of getting at the criteria and judgments of the people within the community regarding social status. In addition, the evaluated participation method translates the criteria and judgments of the townspeople into explicit and verifiable results, conditions necessary for comparative study of the same community in time, or of two or more different communities. Since the final authorities on the reality of any social class structure are the people who live and participate in it, so states Warner, the evaluated participation method safeguards the investigator against imposing his own conception of ranking upon the people and the community he studies.[19]

Hollingshead also was concerned with developing a method which would "utilize local values to define position, standing, or class...."[20] In Hollingshead's study of Elmtown's youth, his working hypothesis was that "the social behavior of adolescents appear to be related functionally to the positions their families occupy in the social structure of the community."[21] After investigations in Elmtown, Hollingshead concluded that a family's position or standing in the social structure depends on not one but a number of socio-cultural characteristics.[22] Hollingshead called his approach to studying social stratification the *rater method*.[23]

The evaluated participation and the rater methods are quite similar in many respects. They are based on somewhat similar assumptions, and each has as its purpose the delineation of differential strata in the social system of a community as the community people have so defined the stratification hierarchy. As a matter of fact, Hollingshead compared the two methods on a segment of Elmtown's population and found that "the two stratification techniques as used by independent investigators produced a valid and reliable index of stratification...."[24] One hundred and thirty-four families status-typed by the Hollingshead rater method in 1941 were status-typed by the Warner evaluated participation method in 1943. The separate and independent studies revealed a 100 percent correspondence for families in Class I, 89 percent agreement for Class II, 83 percent agreement for Class III, 72 percent agreement for Class IV, and 77 percent agreement for Class V families.[25]

As well as these two methods appear to identify the different strata within a community, they are nevertheless cumbersome, time consuming, and require data the acquisition of which involves resources greater than those at the disposal of most investigators. In short, the evaluated participation and rater methods are so elaborate that they are impractical. Warner recognized this problem and attempted to solve it by developing an *index of status characteristics* consisting of four characteristics chosen because "they correlate highly with class and because they are easily obtained and capable of exact comparison among all American communities".[26] Hollingshead developed an *index of social position* consisting of three factors which reflect the social values on which the horizontal strata are based.[27]

In the index of status characteristics, individual or family measurements are taken on a seven point scale for each of the following four status factors -- occupation, source of income, house type, and dwelling area. A weight is assigned to each characteristic which indicates the importance of that particular factor in the prediction of social status. The following weights were assigned: occupation 4, source of income 3, house type 2, dwelling area 3. Measurements on each of these status characteristics are multiplied by the appropriate weight and then totaled to indicate the socio-economic standing of an individual. Warner looks upon these four characteristics as "evaluated symbols which are signs of status telling us the class levels of those who possess the symbols."[28]

The Hollingshead instrument consists of three factors -- ecological area of residence, occupation, and education, and are measured on a six or seven point scale. Weights assigned to these status factors by Hollngshead were: ecological area of residence 5, occupation 8, and education 6. Measurements on the three status characteristics are multiplied by the appropriate weight and then summed. The resultant score is an index of one's position in the community's social class system. Hollingshead states that "the horizontal strata...are based upon the social values that are attached to occupation, education, place of residence in the community, and associations."[29] Clearly, occupation is considered to have higher predictive value of one's social status than any of the other variables used in the index of status characteristics or the index of social position. While house type is represented as having the least predictive value in the index of status characteristics, dwelling area and source of income are asserted to be of equal value, although less significant than occupation. According to the weighting scheme used in the index of social position, area of residence and education are more or less equal, with education showing slightly more predictive value but less than occupation.

It should be mentioned that weights attached to each status factor were derived statistically with the aid of regression equations. There is lack of consensus on the mathematical validity of many of the weighting procedures currently used. To weight or not to weight, therefore, is an open question. Paul Horst edited a book on *Prediction of Personal Adjustment* which carries an article by Marion Richardson relating the experience of correlating two series of tests, each containing 100 items; this experience is reported in relation to the problem of weighting:

Two different composites of items were weighted by means of dice throws; each item thus received a weight of 1 to 6 in each of the composites. The two sets of weights were uncorrelated. [However,] the correlation between the scores on two 100-item tests was approximately .98. It is... recommended that items of a test be assigned weights of unity and it is suggested that little will be gained by the use of elaborate weighting systems.[30]

Factor analysis and other techniques of deriving weights have been proposed. But insufficient evidence make it impossible to conclusively recommend the use of one or another weighting scheme at the present.

If we may agree to lay the weighting problem aside for the moment, let us return to an examination of specific factors proposed as socio-economic indices. Warner assumed that the index of status characteristics was only an approximation of one's evaluated participation. Hence, the evaluated participation measure was used as the criterion of validity for the simplified index of status characteristics. Accepting Warner's assumption, Paul Hatt extended Warner's analysis to determine the minimum number of factors of which the index of status characteristics could consist and still maintain a high correlation with the evaluated participation measure. Hatt observed that a correlation coefficient of approximately .96 could be obtained between the evaluated participation scores and the index of status characteristics when the latter was composed of a combination of factors presented in either of the following two sets: (a) occupation, house type, and *source of income;* or (b) occupation, house type, and *dwelling area.* In fact, Hatt discovered that "occupation alone had a zero order coefficient of correlation with the [evaluated participation measures] of .91."[31] To raise the coefficient of correlation to a point near .95 a combination of factors is necessary. According to Hatt, an effective index for the mass society, or an instrument for cross-community research may be obtained by combining occupation, source of income, and rental value which would allow a correlation with the evaluated participation measures of approximately .95. Hatt rejects house type and dwelling area as status factors because "[they] are expressed in terms of the local community and this impairs their value as cross-community indexes."[32] On the other hand, he incorporates source of income, occupation, and rental value in this index because the first two factors are generalizable -- that is, "we have common sense agreement that source of income is constant as a value throughout our society" and studies of the National Opinion Research Center "indicate an extraordinary amount of agreement on the prestige value of occupations, regardless of region or size of community."[33] Hatt further states that rental is used in the instrument suggested because "it has become accepted as a general principle by ecologists that rental values or rental equivalents are stable and reliable indexes of both the quality of housing and the quality of neighborhood."[34] In the interest of parsimony, Hatt finally suggests that the laborious and expensive community reputation analysis might well be supplanted by "a prestige scale of occupation plus a simple rental index."[35]

In the same journal in which Hatt published his analysis of census tract data of twenty cities of comparable size, Calvin Schmid set forth some generalizations concerning the ecology of the American city based on his analysis of census tract data in twenty cities of comparable size. Intercorrelating some twelve indices, Schmid arrived at the following conclusion: "Educational status shows high positive correlation with mean rent...occupation, and employment status."[36] In differentiating residential areas, Schmid, therefore, recommends some of the following indices as being more satisfactory: (1) median grade completed, (2) mean rent, (3) laborers, (4) college graduates, (5) professional workers, (6) persons unemployed.[37]

There is lack of complete agreement on indices

which should be used to denote socio-economic status of areas. In addition to those mentioned above, other single factors or combination of factors have been proposed. Genevieve Knupfer states in her doctoral dissertation that "approximate rent is the best index of general status."[38] She goes on to say that general stratification indices are interchangeable and that one may choose from among a large number of socio-economic variables for cross-tabulation against a third factor (like voting behavior) without materially changing one's findings.[39]

Part of the difficulty in achieving a consensus on specific socio-economic indices is a problem of conceptualization. Statements about social class, social status, status group, and status aggregate abound in the literature; sometimes these concepts are used interchangeably, indicating that these different phrases refer to or conceptualize the same phenomenon. Some scientists, however, are careful to make fine distinctions between these concepts. Also some social scientists label the same phenomenon with different terms. An illustration of this is seen in the excerpts which follow. Allison Davis states that:

People are of the same class when they may normally (1) eat or drink together as a social ritual, (2) freely visit one another's family, (3) talk together intimately in a social clique, or (4) have cross-sexual access of one another ouside of the kinship group.[40]

This conception is also shared by Warner who states that "social class involves the social participation and social reputation of individuals in the community."[41] He further asserts that "members of a class tend to marry within their own order."[42] On the other hand, Kurt Mayer describes activities almost the same as those outlined by Davis and Warner, but indicates that they denote status rather than class. According to Mayer:

Individuals who occupy a similar position in the status hierarchy of a local community tend to form status groups; that is, they treat each other as social equals, encouraging the intermarriage of their children, joining the same clubs and associations, and par-ticipating together in such informal activities as visiting, dances, dinners, and receptions....[43]

Marriages, dining invitations, friendly participation in recreational activities, clique, and club associations occur among members of the same social class as seen by Davis and Warner, while the same actions are engaged in by individuals of similar social status, according to Mayer.

The haze in conceptualization becomes more dense when the same author uses the terms status and class interchangeably and then at another time states or implies that they refer to different phenomena. This is very much what one experiences when reading the book by W. Lloyd Warner and associates, *Social Classes in America*. They state that "*class* is vitally significant in marriage and in training children as well as in most social activities of a community. *Status* plays a decisive role in the formation of personality at the various stages of development...."[44] (Italics mine.) In the preceding quotation, Warner and associates refer to class and status interchangeably as significantly influencing socialization. In another portion of Warner's work, however, distinction is made between class and status. He asserts that social class involves evaluated participation and social reputation,[45] while characteristics such as occupation, source of income, house type, and dwelling area are indices or symbols of socio-economic status and may be regarded only as an estimate of social class.[46] Pfautz and Duncan, after an extensive review of the literature on stratification, observe that the concept -- class -- is usually treated with two quite different approaches. They say that "many theorists [tend] to consider class relative to the distribution of *power* in the economic and/or political sense, [while] on the other hand, much stratification theory and research centers on the phenomenon of *prestige,* classes being located relative to a hierarchy of esteem rather than power."[47]

To continue this discussion on conceptualization, Stone and Form reject the view that social stratification is a pervasive, integrating, and inclusive structure with respect to community organization. They point out the appropriateness of a multi-dimensional approach in which "social stratification may be apprehended as co-existing in community organization along the lines suggested by Max Weber's proposed social, economic and political orders."[48] Wendell Bell, influenced by the work of Eshref Shevky, hypothesized that "economic status, family status and ethnic status, each, represent a discrete social factor which is necessary to account for the differences between urban sub-populations with respect to social characteristics."[49] Prior to Bell's publications, Shevky and Williams used these dimensions (labeled differently) as bases for organizing their urban community data. Shevky and Williams present these dimensions of community organization as notions derived from observation.[50] Kurt Mayer, too, sanctions a multi-dimensional approach when he describes class, status, and power as three dimensions of stratification. He goes on to say that "the relationship between the distribution of power, class structure, and status hierarchy is highly dynamic, although in stable periods most people occupy quite similar positions in all three hierarchies, and the three dimensions overlap closely."[51]

The guide lines for research into community stratification using the multi-dimensional approach are only dimly sketched, and one hardly knows where to start. The Shevky and Williams studies, and subsequently those by Bell which deal with the dimensions of economic status, family status, and ethnic status are promising but not conclusive; much more research is needed. Hence, these studies may be regarded only as important beginning points.

Much of the progress in clarifying social stratification theory and methodology has occurred in the "re-

jection department." Those factors which serve to further befuddle the task of social science analysis are being cast out. Bell's recent hypothesis regarding ethnicity as a separate dimension of stratification whose
variability does not depend entirely on socio-economic
factors brings to mind the fact that ethnicity for many
years was thought to be a necessary factor in any composite socio-economic index which sought to differentiate a community in a hierarchial fashion. As late as
1939, for instance, Homer Hoyt recommended the
variable -- percentage of non-white persons -- as one of
eight factors most pertinent in revealing housing conditions and throwing most light upon residential areas
with respect to one another.[52]

Since most ethnic groups during the early years of
urban America inhabited the deteriorated and
blighted section of cities, the proportion of persons in
any or all ethnic groups was thought to be an effective
differentiating variable to include in a composite index
of socio-economic stratification. This conclusion usually was arrived at by imputing a causation to an observed association. The fallacy of this practice is revealed
by some of the findings of Jerome Myers who has done
considerable research on the occupational and residential mobility of Italians in New Haven. Since movement by Italian families out of the area of deteriorated
housing into neighborhoods of higher status has consistently lagged far behind their corresponding movement up in the occupational system, Myers observes
that "strictly economic factors are not solely responsible...and that the factor of income alone cannot account for the differences."[53] Multiple factors such as
dominant group values, attitudes, and practices,
minority group desires, aspirations, and experiences,
and available community opportunities as well as
economic considerations enter into the determination
of the geographic locations of ethnic groups.[54] Thus,
ethnicity is judged to be unreliable as an ecological

variable of socio-economic stratification because it may
vary *with* or *independently* of other factors of economic
organization. While it is not clear yet just how much
stratification theory will benefit from research based
on the hypothesis that ethnicity is a separate and independent dimension of community organization, one
may conclued that its rejection as a major factor in the
hierarchial delineation of socio-economic strata is a
refinement in methodology, a refinement which is il-
lustrated in Hollingshead's study of New Haven. He
looked for both vertical and horizontal differentiation
in the community's structure and found differentiation
vertically along racial, ethnic, and religious lines with
each vertical cleavage in turn being differentiated
horizontally by a series of strata which were based upon
social values pertaining to occupation, education,
residential area, and asociations.[55] It is suggested in the
Hollingshead analysis of New Haven that racial,
religious, and nationality ethnic groups constitute
separate structures within the community transected
horizontally by strata which are based on values some
of which appear to be common to all structures. According to Hollingshead, "the New Haven community is a
parallel class structue within the limits of race, ethnic
origin, and religion."[56] Ethnicity, therefore, is omitted
as a determinant of social status in the Hollingshead
scheme.

The developmental process usually involves taking
in and casting out, putting on and throwing off.
Deciding on that which is unnecessary is a useful task.
But the growth of any discipline or science thrives on
new propositions advanced, examined, tested and
verified. Through the haze of entangled ideas, notions,
hypotheses, principles, and theories pertaining to
socio-economic stratification, rays of consensus are
beaming brighter and brighter on one factor that is
considered to be the greatest of them all in effecting
one's position in the stratification hierarchy. This fac-

tor is occupation. Most studies of stratification published since 1940 have mentioned the significance of occupation. Perhaps this is because "occupation rather
than the ownership of property is the main source of income for the overwhelming majority of the population
in the United States."[57] Be that as it may, here are
some generalizations made by scientists who have worked intensively with occupational data. On the level of
the mass society, Hatt states that there is an extraordinary amount of agreement throughout the nation on
the prestige value of different occupations.[58] In terms
of total community typology, Gillen believes that an
occupational index indicates the overall worth of a city
because it sheds light on the general education level
and standard of living.[59] Both Warner and Hollingshead award occupation larger weights in their
composite indexes, showing that it is more significant
in determining social position in the stratification
hierarchy. Shevky and Williams observe that "modern
society is organized on an occupational basis."[60] Ways
in which interpersonal relations like visiting and par-
ticipating in voluntary associations are affected by the
kind of work one usually performs are shown by Floyd
Dotson.[61] North and Hatt state that "one's daily habits
are...determined by the kind of job he holds."[62] A few
statements have been given to illustrate the thinking of
social scientists regarding the factor of occupation in
relation to community and social organization.

Otis and Beverly Duncan have examined the
social ecology of occupation groups to see if principles
derived from this kind of analysis correspond with
those resulting from other methods of study. They conclude that spatial distances between occupation groups
are closely related to their social distances.[63] Studies in
Chicago and in other cities reveal that the most
residentially segregated occupation groups are those at
the extremes of the socio-economic scale. Knowledge
about "differences in occupational background," ac-

cording to Otis and Beverly Duncan, "leads to accurate, specific predictions of the pattern of differences
in residential distribution."[64] In fact, knowledge of a
person's occupation will enable one to predict the kind
of residential neighborhood in which that individual
lives more accurately than would be possible either
with knowledge of a person's income or education.[65]
These inferences drawn by Otis and Beverly Duncan
are based on a census tract and zone-sector analysis of
employed males in Chicago for eight major occupations reported in the 1950 census.

Similar ecological variables may show different
relationships to each other in cities of different size.
Data from Wendell Bell's analysis of Los Angeles and
this investigator's study of Syracuse may be used to illustrate the problem. One factor in Bell's family index
is single-family dwelling units. He states that "the implicit assumption made by Shevky and Williams is that
this measure along with the other two summarized in
the index of family status represents a single continuum
and a different continuum from that measured by the
index of economic status."[66] Occupation, education,
and rent are consolidated in the index of economic
status for the Los Angeles study. Approximations of
these variable were computed for Syracuse. The
numbers of single-family dwelling units by census
tracts had a different relationship to education, occupation, and rent variables in Syracuse than was
found in Los Angeles. In Los Angeles with several
millions of people, one finds little or not correlation
between the distribution of single-family dwellings and
occupation, education, and rent indices by census
tracts. But in Syracuse, New York where there are less
than a quarter of a million people, a definite association exists between the distribution pattern of single-
family homes and such socio-economic factors as occupation, education, and rent. Not a single correlation
coefficient in Syracuse is below .60 for these variables

while in Los Angeles only one factor -- occupation --shows a minimal association at .37; the other two variables yield correlation coefficients of less than .10, suggesting almost no relationship. Based on his analysis of Los Angeles, Bell affirms the assumption of Shevky and Williams. The Syracuse data indicate that this finding in Los Angeles should not be generalized. Additional evidence of the lack of universal disassociation between house type (of the family status index) and other factors such as education and occupation is found in a study published by Hochbaum and associates at the University of Minnesota. Correlating selected urban characteristics for Minneapolis and then comparing them with correlation coefficients reported in Warner's study of Jonesville a much smaller and different kind of community, they found the following: (1) education and house type .32 in Minneapolis; education and house type .70 in Jonesville; (2) occupational rating and house type .45 in Minneapolis; occupational rating and house type .71 in Jonesville.[57] Admittedly, data of the studies mentioned above are not comparable in all respects; but enough similarity does exist between the variables and that which they reflect to provide a basis for suggestig that further research is needed to determine whether family status varies with or independently of socio-economic status and the condition under which there is or is not an association.

My own studies have demonstrated that money income is an important life-chance variable, that it affects black and white populations in a way that is significantly different from the way they are affected by other socio-economic variables. Even when socio-economic factors are the same, there is variation within a status category by income. An ecological study in a middle-sized American city of infant mortality revealed a Pearsonian correlation coefficient of only .53 between median income by census tracts and a five-factor socio-economic status index, consisting of housing, education and occupation variables.[69] With only about one-fourth of the variance in income accounted for by socio-economic status, I have always attempted to isolate income and study its direct contribution to the way of life of a population. Income should not be assumed to have a similar effect as all other socio-economic variables.

By isolating the effect of income, I discovered a critical income level in my infant mortality studies, above which there was little association between neonatal mortality and family finances and below which there was an indirect and significant effect. The concept of a critical income level is an important one to emphasize. Recognition of it helps one to realize how faulty projections can be when the adaptations of individuals in one income category are projected upon individuals in another. For example, above the poverty line income variations of several thousand dollars may not make a difference in the generally low-rate of neonatal mortality for these families. If an affluent population were the only one examined, one might conclude that more or less money is of little consequence so far as the probability of infant death during the first month after birth is concerned. Such a conclusion would be wrong if applied to all income groups. Below the poverty line, a significant variation in this life-chance variable is found among families whose income may differ by only five or six hundred dollars.[70]

Research thus far has resulted in high agreement (though short of unanimity) on occupation, education, residential area, value of dwelling, source and amount of income, and type of dwelling structure as significant variables of neighborhood differentiation. There is an increasing tendency for social scientists to perceive the stratification hierarchy as a system or structure with many dimensions, of which socio-economic status is only one. To date, no one has satisfactorily described all of the multi-dimensions or demonstrated successfully of the multi-dimensions or demonstrated successfully how, if at all, they are integrated into a single system. Happily, however the period of the pot-pourri composite socio-economic index has passed and scientists are advancing, defining, and refining hypotheses which underly the nomination of one or another factor for inclusion in an index of stratification. The early empirical and strictly descriptive ecological studies were of value. They revealed associations between social variables. Hypotheses were later formulated concerning the conditions under which these associations might occur and these hypotheses have served to guide research of an experimental nature.

As an epilogue to this discussion, it should be pointed out that most of our advancements have occurred in the determination of what is not an appropriate indicator of socio-economic stratification. One should not be discouraged, however. For this pattern of growth is sociological knowledge is very much akin to developments in other sciences. One is reminded of genetic experiments with the fruit fly in which investigators sought to determine ways of increasing its life span. To date, however, experimental scientists have learned ways of shortening a fruit fly's life by certain types of cross breeding. As Carlson and Stieglitz put it in their article on "Physiological Changes in Aging," "science has as yet been able only to degrade rather than to strengthen the genetic constitution by experimental means."[68] Even among humans, we have not discovered how to lengthen life so much as we have understood that which interferes with healthful existence. Casting out the wrong, discharging the useless and unnecessary are, therefore, important tasks in social science and contribute much to its growth and development.

On the basis of this review and other data about the system of social stratification in the United States, I make these assertions:

1.   The system of social stratification has both horizontal and vertical dimensions, with the horizontal dimension being class-like in character, having to do with categories of behavior, and the vertical dimension being caste-like in character, having to do with groups or categories of people.

2.   At this period in American history, the important social-class or horizontally differentiated variables are occupation, education and income; they are interrelated but not identical or interchangeable; each can have a unique and different pattern of variation within a category of people of the vertical dimension of the system of social stratification.

3.   At this time in American society, the important social-caste or vertically differentiated categories are race or ethnicity, sex, and age; they are interrelated but not identical or interchangeable; the components of each category such as, for example, blacks, browns and whites, or males and females, or younger, middle-aged, and older people, can have a unique and different pattern of variation with any of the behavioral components of social class of the horizontal dimension of the system of social stratification.

This review helps us to understand some of the problems in Wilson's analysis in *The Declining Significance of Race*. These will be discussed in greater detail in subsequent chapters and are only mentioned here. He gave himself the task of examining a vertical category of the stratification system, race, in relation to social class that is differentiated horizontally. However, his analysis of race was incomplete in that he focused largely on blacks and did not comprehend the different patterns of variations of social class variables among majority and minority members of racial populations. Moreover, Wilson clearly misunderstood the caste-like character of the vertical dimension of the stratification system.

Although Wilson's analysis was of social class, he

gave most attention to only one variable, occupation, which of course is an important component of horizontal differentiation. But this review has revealed that education and income are important social-class variables too. In his analysis, Wilson mentioned education but not in sufficient depth to increase one's understanding of its differential pattern of variation in majority and minority racial populations. Income was almost ignored in the Wilson study. Thus our understanding of the interaction between social class and race is incomplete because Wilson considered only one of the three important social-class variables. The review has demonstrated that each of these is a unique variable and is not interchangeable.

Finally, Wilson comes close to commiting an error of the past--of conceptualizing race as part of the horizontal dimension of the stratification system. He implied that increase in opportunities for racial minorities almost automatically resulted in a decrease in the amount of discrimination that they experienced. Discrimination due to social caste is not the same as differentiation due to social class. One has to do with a category of people while the other is concerned with a component of behavior. A population may experience increased differentiation by social class without experiencing decreased differentiation by social caste.

The critical income level is not the same for all life-chance variables and for these as they are manifested in minority and majority groups. For this reason, it is important to specify the life-chance variables that one is studying. Family composition in black and white families by household income level is such a phenomenon. In examining census data for my book on *A New Look at Black Families*, I discovered that an indirect association existed between family income and family stability as indicated by the presence or absence of two parents in the household; as the family income decreased, the proportion of families headed by one parent increased. This pattern held for blacks and whites. At the affluent end of the income range there was almost no difference in the large number of two-parent households in both races. More than 90 out of every 100 were stable. Below the poverty line, however, the proportion of single-parent households -- which is a majority of the poor in both races -- was nearly one and one-half times greater among blacks compared with whites. The critical income level at which the proportion of single-parent families appeared to increase and involve more than one out of every two households was at the working class or moderate income level for blacks but not until one reached the lower class or poverty level for whites (Willie, 1976:3-4).[71]

Thus, the critical income level may differ not only for different life-chance variables, it may differ for the *same variable* in different races. Beyond providing evidence of why the life-chance variables under study should be specified, this analysis provides information on the distortions that can result from projecting the experience of one population upon another. Finally this review of past research demonstrates the validity of a comparative analysis that recognizes the different existential histories of majority and minority groups and the adaptations that they call forth.

FOOTNOTES FOR CHAPTER 2

1.   C. P. Loomis, J.A. Beegle and T. W. Longmore, *Crtique of Class as Related to Social Stratification* (Beacon House: Beacon House Publishing Co.,

1948), p. 3.
2. Kurt B. Mayer, *Class and Society* (Garden City: Doubleday and Co., 1955), p. 4.
3. Harold F. Kaufman, "An Approach to the Study of Urban Stratification," *American Sociological Review*, XVII (August, 1952), 430.
4. Cecil C. North and Paul K. Hatt, "Jobs and Occupations: A Popular Evaluation," *Sociological Analysis*, ed. Logan Wilson and William Kolb (New York: Harcourt, Brack, and Co., 1949), p. 464.
5. F. H. Finch and A. J. Hoehm, "Measuring Socio-Economic or Cultural Status: A Comparison of Methods," *The Journal of Social Psychology*, XXXIII, (February, 1951), 53.
6. Ernest W. Burgess, "The Growth of the City," *The City*, ed. Robert E. Park, Ernest W. Burgess and Roderick D. McKenzie (Chicago: The University of Chicago Press, 1925), pp. 47-62.
7. Maurice R. Davie, "Patterns of Urban Growth," *Studies in the Science of Society*, ed. George Peter Murdock (New Haven: Yale University Press, 1937), pp. 133-162.
8. Homer Hoyt, *The Structure and Growth of Residential Neighborhoods in American Cities* (Washington: U. S. Government Printing Office, 1939).
9. Ernest W. Burgess, *op. cit.*, p. 55.
10. Murray Leiffer, "A Method for Determining Local Urban Community," *Publications of the American Sociological Society*, XXVI (August, 1932), 137-43.
11. H. W. Green, "Cultural Areas in the City of Cleveland," American Journal of Sociology, XXXVIII (November, 1932), 356-67.
12. Stuart A. Queen, "The Ecological Study of Mental Disorders," *American Journal of Sociology* V (April, 1940), 201-09.
13. W. Lloyd Warner and Paul S. Lunt, *The Social Life of a Modern Community* (New Haven: Yale University Press, 1941).
14. W. Lloyd Warner, Marcia Meeker and Kenneth Eells, *Social Class in America* (Chicago: Science Research Associates, Inc., 1949).
15. August B. Hollingshead, *Elmstown's Youth* (New York: John Wiley and Sons, Inc., 1949).
16. August B. Hollingshead and Frederick C. Redlich, "Social Stratification and Psychiatric Disorders," *American Sociological Review*, XVIII (April, 1953), 163-69.
17. Warner *et al.*, *Social Class in America*, p. 35.
18. *Ibid.*, pp. 37-38.
19. *Ibid.*
20. Hollingshead, *Elmtown's Youth*, pp. 27-28.
21. *Ibid.*, p. 9.
22. *Ibid.*, p. 26.
23. *Ibid.*, pp. 33-36.
24. *Ibid.*, p. 41.
25. Warner *et al.*, *Social Class in America*, p. 40.
26. *Ibid*
27. Hollingshead and Redlich, *American Sociological Review*, XVIII, No. 2, p. 165.
28. Warner *et al.*, *Social Class in America*, p. 40.
29. Hollingshead and Redlich, *American Sociological Review*, XVIII, No. 2, p. 165.
30. Marion Richardson, "The Combination of Measures," *Prediction of Personal Adjustment*, ed. Paul Horst (New York: Social Science Research Council, 1941), 379-401.
31. Paul K. Hatt, "Stratification in the Mass Society," *American Sociological Review*, XV (April, 1950), 221.

32.   *Ibid.*, p. 222.
33.   *Ibid.*
34.   *Ibid.*
35.   *Ibid.*
36.   Calvin F. Schmid, "Generalizations Concerning the Ecology of the American City," *American Sociological Review*, XV (April, 1950), 280.
37.   *Ibid.*
38.   Genevieve Knupfer, "Indices of Socio-Economic Status: A Study of Some Problems of Measurement," (Ph. D. dissertation, Department of Political Science, Columbia University, 1946), p. 107.
39.   *Ibid.*, p. 118.
40.   Allison Davis, *Children of Bondage* (Washington: American Council on Education, 1940), p. 201.
41.   Warner *et al.*, *Social Class in America*, p. 42.
42.   Warner and Lunt, *Social Life of A Modern Community*, p. 82.
43.   Mayer, *op. cit.*, p. 24.
44.   Warner *et al.*, *Social Class in America*, p. 24.
45.   *Ibid.*, p. 42.
46.   *Ibid.*, p. 41.
47.   Harold W. Pfautz and Otis Dudley Duncan, "A Critical Evaluation of Warner's Work in Community Stratification," *American Sociological Review*, XV (April, 1950), 210.
48.   Gregory P. Stone and William H. Form, "Instabilities in Status: The Problem of Hierarchy in the Community Study of Status Arrangements," *American Sociological Review*, XVIII (April, 1953), 150.
49.   Wendell Bell, "Economic, Family, and Ethnic Status: An Empirical Test," *American Sociological Review*, XX (February, 1955), 45.
50.   Eshref Shevky and Marilyn Williams, *The Social Areas in Los Angeles* (Berkeley: University of California Press, 1949).
51.   Mayer, *op. cit.*, p. 27.
52.   Hoyt, *op. cit.*, pp. 26, 34.
53.   Jerome K. Myers, "Assimilation to the Ecological and Social Systems of a Community," *American Sociological Review*, XV (June, 1950). 372.
54.   *Ibid.*, p. 371.
55.   Hollingshead and Redlich, *American Sociological Review*, XVIII, No. 2, p.165.
56.   *Ibid.*
57.   Mayer, *op. cit.*, p. 31.
58.   Hatt, *op. cit.*, p. 222.
59.   Paul Bates Gillen, *The Distribution of Occupations as a City Yardstick* (New York: King's Crown Press of Columbia University, 1951), pp. 107-113.
60.   Shevky and Williams, *op. cit.*, p. 38.
61.   Floyd Dotson, "Patterns of Voluntary Association Among Urban Working-Class Families," *American Sociological Review*, XVI (October, 1951), 687-693.
62.   North and Hatt, *op. cit.*, p. 464.
63.   Otis Dudley Duncan and Beverly Duncan, "Residential Distribution and Occupational Stratification," *The American Journal of Sociology*, LX (March, 1955), 502.
64.   *Ibid.*
65.   *Ibid.*, p. 500.
66.   Bell, *op. cit.*, p. 46.
67.   Godfrey Hochbaum *et al.* "Socio-Economic Variables in a Large City," *The American Journal of Sociology*, LXI (July, 1955), 34.
68.   Anton J. Carlson and Edward J. Stieglitz, "Physiological Changes in Aging,"

The Annals CCLXXIX (January, 1952), 20.

69.   Charles V. Willie, "A Research Note on the Changing Association between Infant Mortality and Socio-Economic Status," *Social Forces,* 37 (March, 1959), pp. 221-227.

70.   Charles V. Willie and William B. Rothney, "Racial, Economic and Income Factors in the Epidemiology of Neonatal Mortality," *American Sociological Review,* 27 (August, 1962), pp. 522-526.

71.   Charles V. Willie, *A New Look at Black Families,* Bayside, New York: General Hall, 1976, pp. 3-4.

3

RELATIVE EFFECT OF RACE AND
SOCIAL CLASS ON FAMILY INCOME*

I must begin this chapter with a confession. I cannot find anywhere data that confirm William Wilson's conclusion that "the more talented and highly educated blacks are experiencing unprecedented job opportunities in the corporate and government sector because of the expansion of salaried white collar positions and the pressures of demonstrated affirmative action" (p. 121). The AT and T court case about race and sex discrimination in hiring, training, and promoting already has been mentioned. The experience of that industry is not unlike that of many others.

In addition, I can find no data that make it difficult for me "to comprehend the economic plight of lower class blacks in the inner city by focusing solely on racial oppression" (p.120).

Moreover, authorities in demography and economics that I have consulted such as Herman Miller, formerly of the Census Bureau, state that "race

*Enlarged version of discussion with William Wilson at Michigan State University, East Lansing, Michigan, November 16, 1978

discrimination is a key cause" of the black's perpetual low estate (Herman Miller, "The Dimensions of Poverty" in Ben Seligman, *Poverty as a Public Issue*, New York: Free Press, 1965, p. 21).

Consider this interview between one of the field workers in Hylan Lewis' Child Rearing Study in the Washington, D.C. area in the 1960s:

Interviewer: Do you have any blacks working under you?

Foreman: No. Right now we are building a house for an army colonel. We never use blacks in jobs in the suburban area because that would hurt the company's reputation.

Interviewer: Do you ever use blacks?

Foreman: When we have a job in Washington, we hire a large number of blacks.

Interviewer: Why?

Foreman: The black painter is able and willing to do the same job for only half the pay of a white painter. Give me a crew of six niggers and we'll knock out a five-story office building in a week. They all got families and half pay is damn good money for a nigger (Charles V. Willie, *A New Look at Black Families*, Bayside, N.Y.: General Hall, 1976, p. 175).

Now William Wilson might protest that these are old data, that whites do not discriminate against blacks this way anymore because the 1964 Civil Rights Act;and Affirmative Action regulations prohibit such discrimination.

Because William Wilson's analysis baffles me, rather than argue with him about his data that I do not understand, I decided to make my own analysis using data that are accessible to all of us. In the Current Populations Reports, Series P-60, No. 114, the Bureau of the Census issued a study entitled *Money Income in 1976 of Families and Persons in the United States*. On pages 143 and 145 of this report it is clearly indicated that the median family income of heads of households

was $12,199 for blacks and other racial minorities and
$17,228 for whites. As late as the Bicentennial Year in
the United States, the median for racial minorities was
only 71 percent of that received by whites. Moreover, a
trend analysis of median family income that was
published by the U.S. Office of Management and
Budget under the title *Social Indicators, 1973* revealed
that black and other racial minority families have been
receiving 30 percent less income than white families for
nearly a decade (p. 146).

It was not the Civil Rights Act of 1964 that
upgraded the economic condition of blacks over-all to
within 30 percentage points of the median annual income of whites. It was the death of Martin Luther
King, Jr., in 1968 that, in my judgment, shamed the
nation into a few new steps toward the goal of equity.
In 1967, black families received 66 percent as much income as whites received. The year in which Martin
Luther King, Jr., died, blacks inched forward four
percentage points and received 70 percent as much income as did whites. Before 1968, median family income for blacks and other racial minorities had varied
from 61 to 67 percent during the previous decade.
Now, it has held constant during the 1970s at 70 to 71
percent and has varied very little. One could say, on
the basis of these data, that the sacrificial death of
Martin Luther King, Jr., brought blacks and other
racial minorities five percentage points closer to income equity with whites but left the nation 30 percentage points still short of the goal.

William Wilson contends that these analyses of
total populations mask too much, that we must look at
the super affluent and those who are really poor. I did
this and used 1976 data from the Census Bureau report
on *Money Income in 1976 of Families and Persons in
the United States.* I found that professional blacks and
those in technical and managerial positions did better
than those who were service workers. A majority of

blacks and other racial minorities in service work are in cleaning and food-handling jobs which are among the lowest paid jobs in the economy. For example, the median family income for blacks in professional and technical work was $17,286 in 1976. The median was nearly twice as great as the $8,284 median found among racial minorities employed at the bottom of the economic heap (pp. 143, 145).

This analysis of the annual income differential by occupational groups within the race does not indicate how minority and majority racial populations are rewarded when they pursue the same occupations. The latter analysis is essential in determining the relative effect of race (as measured by minority/majority status) and social class (as measured by occupation) on life-chance (as measured by income). As William Wilson has suggested, black professional and managerial workers are doing better than black service workers compared to whites. The annual median family income for heads of households in service work who are black or of other racial minority status is only 67 percent of that received by whites who are similarly employed. Black professional and managerial workers, however, are closer than their blue-collar cousins to parity in median annual income with whites of these occupations, although they miss the goal of equity by as much as 20 percentage points. One could state the facts this way: the United States celebrated its Bicentennial Year with black professional and technical workers at the top of the occupational hierarchy receiving an average of 20 percent less income than whites of similar occupations to support their families. Some might claim that being down one-fifth rather than one-third from the goal of income equity"ain't bad," particularly if one is black. I consider it to be a cruel white trick to urge blacks and other racial minorities to stay in school and improve themselves by becoming educated, to give them the responsibility in-

herent in professional and managerial work, and then
to pay them only 80 percent of what they should get.
One could call this a racial tax that is assessed on all
citizens of the United States who are not white. The income differential between minority and majority racial
populations is significant, as these data reveal. Such
differences are too great to conclude that race is no
longer a significant contributor to the oppression of
blacks.

William Wilson and others might claim that the
analysis of the effect of race on depressing the annual
median family income of blacks compared to whites is
defective because it includes people of older age levels,
some of whom were employed before passage of the
1964 Civil Rights Act and the death of King. This is a
fair claim and it should be examined. Fortunately, the
United States Civil Rights Commission did my work for
me. In a report entitled *Social Indicators of Equality
for Minorities and Women* that was issued in 1978, the
Commission used the statistical technique of multiple
regression analysis to determine whether the problem
of less pay for blacks and other races relative to whites
was a function of different characteristics of these
populations or a function of unequal pay for equal
work (p. 53). The goal of the study was to develop income figures for persons in equivalent situations. The
Survey of income and education is based on 15,170
households, making it one of the largest nondecennial
surveys ever conducted. Most interviews took place during May and June of 1976 (p. 108).

"Statistical adjustments were made by the use of
multiple regression for each minority group's level of
education, level of job prestige, income level of the
state of residence, weeks worked, hours recently worked per week, and age. The hypothetical annual earning figures calculated for each minority...group after
these adjustments can be interpreted as the earnings
that would be received by a member of each group if

the person had the same level of education...etc., as the average [member of the] majority....The hypothetical annual earnings can then be compared to the expected earnings of a [member of the] majority....Because any difference in the resulting adjusted earnings cannot be due to differences in education, [age],...etc., the resulting differences in earning are considered...to be the cost of being...minority" (p. 53).

These were the findings. "The equity indicator values...reveal a high degree of similarity among minority groups and considerable inequity between minority groups and the majority male group" (p. 53).

In 1975, for example, black males with the same characteristics as majority males could be expected to earn 85 percent of the amount that majority males earned. For Mexican-Americans, the equity value was 82 percent. On the basis of this study that was conducted in 1976, one may conclude that even when all things are equal (including age, education, and occupation) black and other minority males receive an annual income that is 15 to 20 percent less than that received by majority white males (p. 54). These findings indicate that racism is alive and well in the United States.

To demonstrate that indeed there is a race tax that is subtracted from the annual income of blacks and other racial minorities and to illustrate in a more simple way the findings derived from the complicated multiple regression analysis that was commissioned by the Civil Rights Commission, I decided to investigate a single occupational category -- that of teachers in elementary and secondary schools. Dorothy Newman *et al.* reported that the median years of school completed (16.6 year for blacks and 16.5 years for whites) was essentially the same for minority and majority group teachers in 1970 (Newman *et al.*, *Protest, Politics and Prosperity*, New York: Pantheon Books,

1978, p. 88). The U.S. Civil Rights Commission used Lloyd Teme's occupational prestige scores and reported that secondary and elementary teachers had similar prestige scores of 63 and 64 respectively (U.S. Civil Rights Commission, p. 96). These scores are on the high side of a range from 1 to 88. The Bureau of the Census reported that about the same proportions of racial minority and majority employed are teachers (2.1 percent for blacks and other races and 2.0 percent for whites). Although blacks and whites in the teaching profession tend to be similarly educated, the median family income for blacks of $13,985 was only 74 percent as great as the $19,009 median for whites.

For all occupations, when differences were controlled for statistically and the analysis was limited to males, blacks paid a 15 percent tax in less income received for not being white. Concerning only the teaching profession which in this analysis, involved both men and women, blacks who were similarly educated as whites received one-quarter less income. This sum could be construed as their tax for not being white. The above analysis presents information that is contrary to William Wilson's conclusion that "the equal employment legislation in the earlier sixties have virtually elimiated the tendency of employers to create a split labor market in which black labor is deemed cheaper than white labor regardless of the work performed..." (William Wilson, *The Declining Significance of Race*, Chicago: University of Chicago Press, p. 110).

We turn now to the issue of whether social class as indicated by level of occupation is more significantly related to family income than is minority or majoritry racial status. Again a comparative analysis is helpful. Professional and technical occupations are among the most prestigious and some service jobs are least prestigious. These two broad categories are appropriate for a social class analysis. The annual median family income for the highest paid whites in 1976 was the $21,925 that was received by the professional, technical and kindred workers; this sum contrasted with the $8,284 annual median income recieved by black employed service workers who were lowest in the occupational hierarchy. A spread of 62 percentage points existed between the median income of the lowest occupational group which incidentally was black and the highest occupational group which was white. One could call this the social-class spread in the income variable. In terms of race, the annual median income for all blacks and other racial minority household heads was $12,199 compared to $17,228 for whites. The racial minority annual family income was 71 percent of the income of the racial majority group; by race, a spread of 29 percentage points existed between the highest and lowest family-income medians.

Thus, the income spread by social class as measured by occupational groups was twice as great as the income spread by race as determined by minority/majority status. Even if the black tax that discounts the income for racial minority families by one-third among service workers were eliminated and the income range for blacks by occupations was the same as that for whites, 44 percentage points still would remain between the median income of the highest and lowest occupational categories. This figure for the social-class groups would continue to be greater than the percentage-point spread between the income medians of majority and minority racial groups. Up to this point in the analysis, one could say that William Wilson's thesis that social class influences the family-income variable more than race is correct; but there is more to come.

It is precisely because William Wilson attributed the gains by blacks as due to affirmative action that I must carry the analysis further. It will be seen that an affirmative action analysis will cancel out even the modest lead that the social-class variable now appears to have over race as exerting a more significant effect on income.

One should remember that a macro-sociological analysis is of what Peter Blau has called "structural parameters" rather than of individuals (Peter M. Blau, "A Macrosocial Theory of Social Structure," *American Journal of Sociology*, vol. 83, July, 1977). Blau concludes that parameters are fundamental characteristics of macro-structures and that they often are interrelated so that a nominal parameter such as race or sex may correlate with a graduated parameter such as occupation. Then he observed that "the degree to which parameters intersect, or alternatively consolidate differences in social positions through their strong correlations, reflect the most important structural conditions in a society which have crucial consequences for conflict and for social integration" (Blau, 1977, p. 32). According to Blau, the basic question in social research is to determine "what independent influences the structure of social positions in a society...exert on social relations" (Blau, 1977, p. 28), and, I would say, vice versa. Affirmative action is a public policy that requires a new kind of relationship with minority and majority racial populations by employers who are recruiting new workers. This relationship could affect the social class structure to such an extent that the relative contribution of social class and race to family income could be changed.

William Wilson states that "the rapid growth of the corporate and government sectors has been the gradual creation of a segmented labor market that currently provides vastly different mobility opportunities for different segments of the black population. On the one hand, poorly trained and educationally limited blacks...see their job prospects increasingly restricted to the low-wage sector....On the other hand, talented and educated blacks are experiencing unprecedented job opportunities in the growing government and corporate sector, opportunities that are at least comparable to those of whites with equivalent qualifications" (Wilson, 1978, p. 151). On the basis of these observations, William Wilson concludes that, "The recent mobility patterns of blacks lend strong support to the view that economic class is clearly more important than race in predetermining job placement and occupational mobility" (Wilson, 1978, p. 152). In a direct and forthright manner, William Wilson states that "life chances of blacks have less to do with race than with economic class affiliation" (Wilson, 1978, p. 152).

William Wilson states that his is a macrosocial analysis but he is not consistent and shifts back and forth between individuals and the total racial population as the unit of analysis. A macrosocial analysis should focus on the nominal parameter, on blacks as a population. If Wilson had done this consistently, his conclusions would have been the opposite of those published.

Race depresses black family income more than social class for blacks. The greatest negative effect for the race is experienced at the top rather than at the bottom of the social class (or occupational) hierarchy. This occurs precisely because of the absence of affirmative employment practices that are designed to achieve equity in the proportions of white and black or other minority professional and managerial workers.

The report, *All Our Children*, by the Carnegie Council presents data by race and income analyzed by Rhona Pavis. She found that "90 percent of the income gap between blacks and whites is the result...of lower pay for blacks with comparable levels of education and experience" (Kenneth Keniston *et al.*, *All Our Children*, New York: Harcourt Brace Javanovich, 1977, p. 92).

I do not know the basis for this conclusion but

decided to make some calculations of my own based on data presented in the Current Population Reports (Series P-60, No. 114, July, 1978) of the U.S. Census Bureau (*Money Income in 1976 in Families and Persons in the United States*). My goal was to determine how much of the total income difference between whites and blacks or other minorities was due to the presence of racial discrimination and the absence of effective affirmative action practices to overcome such discrimination.

By keeping the analysis at the macrosocial level and determining what had happened to the total parameter or population of blacks and other racial minorities, I get the following results. The results are based on these assumptions: (1) that black and other minority household heads should be randomly distributed throughout all occupations so that their percent in any particular category is the same as their percent in the total population of the employed, (2) that the median can be used as the representative income figure that each household received in 1976, (3) that blacks and other racial minorities ought to receive the same median income that whites received.

These are assumptions that affirmative action orders and antidiscrimination laws can be fully effective. On the basis of these assumptions, my calculations revealed that the 4.1 million households that were headed by blacks who were employed for some period of time in 1976 should have received $67.3 billion in annual income rather then $49.7 billion. In 1976, according to my calculations, racial discrimination cost employed blacks and other racial minorities $17.6 billion.

One reason blacks were $17.6 billion down from what they should have received is because affirmative action had not overcome the selective employment practices by race that characterizes American society. In the high paying professional, managerial, sales and skilled-craft jobs, there were only 1.1 million racial minorities when there should have been 2.3 million if there were equity in employment. These high paying jobs in a free and open and equitable society would have contributed two-thirds of the total income received by the population of blacks and other minorities if there were as many racial minorities as there should have been in these high paying jobs; those who manage to get employment in them were paid on the average one-fifth less than whites who held similar positions. Thus, these four high paying occupational categories accounted for only one-third of the total income for blacks and other racial minority households, because of the limitations imposed by racial discrimination.

Unlike the white population in which two-thirds of the income for the group comes from these higher paying jobs, the black population is the opposite and receives two-thirds of its income from the lower status occupations. It is fair to say on the basis of these findings that the black community continues to be supported largely by the wealth of its blue-collar workers. Also, despite the mobility of some educated blacks, the data revealed that only three percent of the managers and administrators came from black or other minority household heads in 1976, that there were two-thirds fewer than there should have been and that, collectively, they earned $9.5 billion less than they would have earned had there not been any discrimination in the number of minorities employed in these occupations and in the salaries that they received. This occupational category showed the highest discrepancy between what was and should have been; it was followed by professional and technical workers where the discrepancy was down $6.9 billion from what it should have been. The depressed income of the white-collar and skilled workers contributed greater to the $17.6 billion income deficit that black and other minorities experienced due to discrimination than did wages received or the overrepresentation in numbers of minorities in blue-collar occupations. From a macrosocial perspective, William Wilson's conclusions are wrong. Since $17.6 billion in 1976 would have come to blacks and other minorities had they not been discriminated against, I must conclude that race is a significant variable and continues to influence the income life-chance of the racial minorities in this nation, including the affluent as well as the poorer sector of the population, and that the economic effect of racial discrimination is greater among the affluent than among the poor.

Finally, let me deal directly with the issue of the poor. William Wilson states that "a comparison of their situation with the unprecedented gains of educated blacks demonstrates, in very sharp relief, the growing class divisions in the black community and the inadequacy of conventional explanations of racial experience" (Wilson "The Declining Significance of Race, Revisited but Not Revised," Society, No. 5, July/August, 1978, p. 19). Further, Wilson states that "class divisions related to greatly different mobility opportunities are growing more rapidly in the black community than in the white community" (Wilson, Society, 1978, p. 20). He makes it clear that the condition of the black poor and ways of overcoming their circumstances are his "primary concern" (Wilson, Society, 1978, p.21). Yet he persists in stating that race is of little consequence and is of little value in explaining the "deleterious physical conditions of the isolated black poor" (Wilson, Society, 1978, p. 21).

With reference to poor blacks and whites who are employed in the lowest status occupations of service work, there is little, if any, difference in the education of blacks and whites who are, for example, barbers, cooks, hairdressers, practical nurses, and waiters. (Newman, 1978, p. 90). Yet the median family income for black and other minority household heads employed in these and other service occupations in 1976 was one-third less than the median income of whites in these same low prestige jobs. If race is not an appropriate explanation, why is it that whites of limited education are paid one-third more than blacks who are as qualified as they are? Newman and associates point out that "Blacks had achieved 94 percent of whites' educational position by 1974 and 1975, compared with 79 percent in 1940. But whatever the year, blacks' occupational position did not match their educational position" (Newman, 1978, p. 49).

There is no evidence, again for employed household heads, of any difference in the stratification hierarchy of black and white workers. The median income for professional and technical workers is slightly more than twice the figure for white service workers. A similar pattern exists among blacks except that the median family income for professional and technical workers is slightly less than twice the figure for black service workers. Thus, the stratification or social class hierarchy (as determined by jobs) is the same for black and white populations in the United States today. What differs between these two groups, despite their similar median education of 12.4 years for whites and 11.1 years for blacks, is the proportions of both populations that are poor. In 1959, for example, 18 percent of white households were headed by individuals who were below the official poverty level compared to 56 percent of the households headed by blacks and other races. In 1976, nearly two decades later, the proportion of poor whites had dropped to the low level of 9 percent. However, blacks below the poverty level constituted 29 percent of their total race. In 1959, blacks below the poverty level were three times greater than the proportion of poor whites; seventeen years later the ratio was the same (Bureau of the Census, *Statistical Abstract, 1977,* Washington, D.C.: U.S. Government Printing Office, 1977, p. 454). As I see it, race discrimination that kept a disproportionate number of blacks below the poverty level in 1959 continued to do this in 1976.

In 1967, before the death of Martin Luther King, Jr., the dropout rate for black youngsters 14 to 17 years of age was twice as great as that for whites; today the dropout rate for these ages in these two populations is the same (Census, *Statistical Abstract* 1977, p. 141). Yet whites with limited education manage to get better jobs than blacks. If this is not due to racial discrimination, I don't know what other explanation is applicable.

Among children of the mid-twentieth century --black or white -- there are few who are illiterate; less than one percent of persons 25 to 34 years of age in either race have received less than five years of schooling. A majority in both races who are 25 years of age and over have attended or graduated from high school. With the gains in education that blacks have made since the midpoint of the century, why do poorly educated whites whose education is comparable to that of blacks continue to get better jobs than blacks, so much so that the ratio of blacks to whites in poverty is the same today as it was in 1959, when a greater discrepancy in schooling existed between the races. Until William Wilson can explain this, he would be wise to drop his contention that social differentiation among blacks is consigning poor blacks to poverty. There is social differentiation to be sure, among blacks as well as whites. And although professionals who are white receive approximately twice as much income as do poor whites, only one out of every 10 whites is poor. Professionals who are black also receive about twice as much income as poor blacks; yet three out of every 10 blacks are poor. The stratification pattern between the two races is similar. What accounts for the difference if race is not significant? William Wilson has not given a satisfactory answer.

Wilson notes that there is increasing differentiation among blacks. By my own reckoning, I would place one-third in the middle class or above, one-third in the working class and about one-third below the poverty line. Class differentiation may or may not be associated with caste diminution. Anyone who has studied American history should recognize this. If Wilson had undertaken a comparative analysis of the races by occupation and income as I did, he would have realized that the greatest under-representation of blacks in terms of number of persons employed and the greatest inequality in terms of income received occured at the top of the occupational and income hierarchy. A comparative analysis of living arrangements also would have revealed that the greatest amount of residential commingling among the races has occurred over the years among the poor rather than the affluent. Albert Simkus' study of ten urbanized areas revealed that "historically, blacks with high income have been as highly or more highly segregated from whites with similar income than have low-income blacks." Beyond a new trend of more racial integration found among professionals, Simkus said "nonwhites and whites in the lowest occupational categories were still slightly less segregated than those in the higher category" (Simkus, 1978). All of this is to say that occupational or social class differentiation may be associated with more or less racial discrimination.

Caste and class are structural parameters. A macrosociological analysis is a study of one of these parameters rather than of individuals (Blau, 1977). It would appear that Wilson veered from the basic requirement of a macrosocial analysis -- that is, the requirement to analyze structural effects and permitted the behavior of individuals to influence his conclusions. Even though a few black professionals or managers, for example, may receive an annual salary that is higher than that received by some whites, the macrosocial analyst must keep in perspective what is happening to the total parameter and what are the structural effects. Despite the fact that there is increased differentiation within the social class parameter for blacks so that a hierarchy of jobs is visible among blacks, this development has not wiped out the inequities between the caste parameters, especially income inequities. Indeed the gap between the minority and majority races in the caste parameters tends to be greater at the higher levels of the class parameter than at lower levels. This phenomenon is the opposite of that suggested by Wilson.

Again, a comparative analysis would have protected Wilson from committing the error of attributing the disproportionate amount of unemployment and economic hardship found among the black poor to the increasing differentiation of the black class structure which, according to him, began to take on "some of the characteristics of the white class structure" after World War II (Wilson, 1978, p. 150). Wilson should remember that the social class parameter among whites has been differentiated for years. Nevertheless, the number of poor people among whites has continued to decrease so that today only about one out of every 10 is below the poverty line compared with three out of every ten blacks. If poverty has been almost eradicated among whites, although that population is differentiated by social class, why cannot it be eliminated among blacks? A differentiated class structure does not require that those at the bottom of the stratification hierarchy should be impoverished.

My conclusion is that the disproportionate rate of poverty among blacks in the United States probably should be attributed more to racial discrimination associated with the caste parameter than to differentiation by social class. Wilson's failure to differentiate between caste and class and to analyze these as nominal and graduate parameters that produce structural effects rather than individual consequences is a major conceptual flaw in his study.

All of this brings me to the bottom line of why I am exercised about William Wilson's exercise that has resulted in his book that concludes that race is declining in significance as a determinant of life-chances. First, his analysis is misleading by presenting information about the success of a few talented and highly educated black individuals as if this represented the experience of the entire parameter. Second, Wilson is fishing in the troubled waters of affirmative action. Since the *Bakke* Supreme Court decision, major institutions throughout the nation have been seeking ways of backing off from fulfilling the requirements of affirmative action. When Wilson states that "the life-chances of individual blacks seem indeed to be based far more on their present economic class position than on their status as black Americans" (Wilson, 1978, p. 111), he gives license to employers to ignore the persisting inequities of American society that are attributable directly to the caste system, such inequities as under employment of minorities in high paying professional and managerial jobs and the lower median income of minorities compared with the majority.

Wilson acknowledges on page 152 of his book that there is "firm white resistance to public school desegregation, residential integration, and black control of central cities." With reference to these resistances, he stated it could be argued that they "indicate the unyielding importance of race in America." So if the "life-chances of blacks have less to do with race" as Wilson contends, obviously he is not talking about life-chances pertaining to the residential area where one may live and the public school which one may attend since in his own words these continue to "indicate the unyielding importance of race."

In his analysis of *The Declining Significance of Race*, Wilson has committed four errors in his approach and these indicate why I think the book is

potentially harmful and should be challenged. Among
the four major errors that are committed: (1) Wilson
presents macrosocial conclusions based on a
microsocial analysis; (2) he does not operationally
define life-chances; (3) he does not present a comparative analysis of the association, if any, between
variations in life-chances within minority and majority populations, and (4) he does not distinguish conceptually between caste and class as social parameters that
have structural effects.

ANALYTICAL COMMENTS

4

GETTING AHEAD
And the Man Behind The Class-Race Furor*

By

Hollie I. West
The Washington Post

This is the tale of a thorny idea, and whether its
time has come. The furor began in the hallowed cor-
ridors of academe and has gone on to involve some of
the nation's leading social scientists.

The argument revolves around whether economic
opportunities for black Americans now are shaped
more by class than race. And some say the fallout could
dramatically touch those who don't keep up with shifts
in percentile income or demographic distinctions.

One side fears the idea's acceptance could wipe
out affirmative action and anti-discrimination programs. The other embraces the idea, feeling the gap
between the black haves and have-nots is widening.

And the man who has fueled the current dispute is
William Julius Wilson, the pipe-smoking, new chair-
man of the sociology department of the University of
Chicago, with his book, "The Declining Significance of

Race."

Class and race, intertwined, and debatable elements in whether Americans "make it" or fall by the wayside, played a key role in the life of Wilson, who struggled to escape the poverty of eastern Pennsylvania's coal fields.

"My father died when I was 13," recalls the 42-year-old scholar, who grew up in Bairdstown, about 50 miles east of Pittsburgh. "All we ever heard from our mother was talk of going to college," he says. "I made it and then served as a role model for my brothers and sisters.

"I know what it is to be poor. After my father died, we [the mother and six children] went on relief, what's called welfare now. But we didn't let that stop us from trying to improve ourselves."

Wilson's hunger for social mobility and excellence have taken him to his present chairmanship, a coveted position because of the department's high standing as a prime training ground for influential sociologists.

Taking Sides

So now Wilson is embroiled in a controversy in which he contends that poorly trained and educationally limited blacks see their job prospects increasingly restricted to the low-wage sector, while talented and educated blacks are experiencing unprecedented job opportunities.

The result, he writes, is that "the recent mobility patterns of blacks lend strong support to the view that economic class is clearly more important than race in predetermining job placement and occupational mobility."

Scholars have lined up for and against Wilson in the unprecedented standoff among black intelectuals. Fourteen members of the 88-member Association of Black Sociologists voted recently to condemn the book as a "misrepresentation of the black experience," claiming that attention given it "obscures the problem of the persistent oppression of blacks." The group also expressed fear that the book may be used to shape government policy.

Wilson supporters say his theories don't mean that race is going out the window but that the sociologist is merely reflecting how increasingly fluid American society has become.

Recently, Wilson debated the idea at Michigan State University with Charles Willie, professor of education and urban studies at Harvard, who charges that Wilson has isolated the "economic sphere from other institutions and social arrangements of society."

Both claim they scored points in front of a predominantly student audience. But Willie had the reservation that most white students don't believe that blacks are discriminated against at white colleges.

Wilson, an indefatigable debater, is trying to stand up under the physical stress and emotional woes of constantly defending his ideas against intellectual heavyweights--and bantamweights. For the last two months, under the rigors of travel and talking, he's been unable to shake a cold.

"It's becoming increasingly difficult for me to get up for debates," he says puffing on his pipe. "I've turned down 10 invitations to lecture in the last two months. I'd like to do more writing and attend to more matters at the office."

But there are some speaking engagements he considers necessary. In March, four social scientists will discuss the book in a critics-meet-the-author session at the annual meeting of the Eastern Sociological Society in New York. That same month the University of Pennsylvania has scheduled a three-day conference on the question of class and race in black America.

'Willing and Ready'

Also, Wilson will speak at several southern black colleges in the spring.

However, like his favorite pro basketball player, Julius (Dr. J) Erving, Wilson likes one-on-one confrontations. "I am willing and ready to debate the issues publicly and I have been doing this for the last several months," he smiles. "And I've got to say I haven't seen a criticism of my book yet that I couldn't handle."

In his unassuming, quiet fashion, Wilson sees himself as a spokesman but not the leader of a cause. "I feel the need to spell out the issues I raised in my book," he smiles. "But I don't feel I've had a need to lead a fight. Sometimes I'd like to go back in the four rooms of my office and write."

A principal antagonist of the Wilson idea is eminent psychologist Kenneth B. Clark, a man active in the intellectual marketplace two decades before Wilson started his career and whose ideas gained international attention when they were used by the U.S. Supreme Court in its 1954 decision outlawing racial segregation in the nation's public schools.

The two were scheduled to debate in October, but Clark had to leave the country for another engagement. Earlier, the psychologist had outlined his opposition in a New York Times op-ed page piece in March.

Wrote Clark: "The Belief that class is now replacing racial distinctions in the present stage of the civil-rights struggle seems to be supported only by the fact that a pitiable few number of blacks are permitted to compete with whites for higher status positions."

The upward mobility of blacks, Clark continued, is dependent on the benevolence of whites who control special uplift programs.

"No black can yet be sure that he is being seen, evaluated and reacted to in terms of his qualities and characteristics as an individual rather than categorized and stereotyped as part of a rejected group," Clark wrote. "Until this is a fact, then racism dominates class achievements in spite of the wishful thinking of black and white liberals, social workers and social scientists."

However, Wilson has his supporters. Nathan Glazer, professor of scoiology at Harvard, says, "I think it's an important book. Some people oppose it because of their emotional investment and the historical factor. Suppose you were to tell Jews that they were killed in Europe because they were capitalists.

"No one is making the claim that race was not important for the past, but things are changing. Wilson's book looks at the present and the future. These are not things that haven't been said before. It is the first time a black social scientist has said them with such strength.

"Of course there is a class-race interplay here which is complicated."

Not Far Enough

Another supporter is William Sampson, professor of sociology and urban affairs at Northwestern University, who says the book was "pretty much on the mark and close to what I said in an article three years ago."

But Sampson doesn't think Wilson went far enough.

"Class is more important than race," he continues. "That's given. But what about the questions of whether class differences have behavioral significance for blacks? Or does this mean the establishment of a permanent black underclass? Or what kind of animosity exists between the black middle class and underclass? What kind of role models will young blacks have?"

Wilson knows firsthand the need for role models. His aunt, Mrs. Janice Wardlaw, a retired psychiatric social worker in New York, filled the requirement. With her encouragement, he went to college and helped his brothers and sisters do the same (all six children have since earned at least a bachelor's degree).

As a youth, Wilson spent his summer in New York with Wardlaw, who has two master's degrees. She recalls: "The very year that Billy finished high school I asked him to come live with us. I used to take him to my office and introduce him to people. My husband introduced him to boy scouting and I took him to museums.

"He and I used to talk a lot about history. I encouraged him to study sociology or political science."

So Wilson has gone on to obtain degrees from Wilberforce, Bowling Green and Washington State, write three books and be named teacher of the year in 1970 at the University of Massachusetts. "The Declining Significance of Race" has won the American Sociological Association's Sydney Spivack Award.

Wilson has entered the middle class, but he denies the criticism that his chief concern is the middle class.

Looking out the window of his office past the ivy-covered ledge, Wilson takes a deep puff on his pipe and speaks in a deliberate cadence: "The real problem in the black community today is the poor, unskilled worker who is faced with unemployment and decreasing job opportunities...

"If people read my book carefully, they will find out that I say that blacks do experience discrimination regardless of their class positions, especially in the areas of housing and education.

"But to suggest that an educated black with a five-figure salary and driving his Mercedes-Benz has an experience similar to a poor black trapped in a ghetto and confined to menial dead-end jobs is stretching the point a bit."

To the criticism that he has isolated the economic sphere from the rest of life, Wilson says he is contending that the economic factor has greater strength in determining life chances.

Wilson maintains that not enough attention is given the poor and that the problems of the underclass cannot be addressed by anti-discrimination and affirmative action programs. He says discrimination and prejudice created the poor, who are particularly vulnerable in social change as society moves from a goods and service producing organism to automation and technology.

Wilson says one antidote is to create more jobs and guarantee full emloyment.

"We need to recognize that affirmative action and anti-discrimination programs are not enough," he explains. "They stop short. They don't deal with the concrete problems gripping poor blacks...

"No one ever said that race is insignificant. I certainly have never said that, but it's quite clear that there's a class factor that's operating."

Nevertheless, in the midst of the debate over his book, Wilson realizes he can't go on interminably arguing his case.

"I'm going to be writing an introduction to 'Declining Significance of Race,' a new epilogue that will consider some of the criticism of the book," he says.

Meanwhile, he says, "I've got to go on to something else, I'd like to write a definitive theoretical general work, something in macro-sociology. That would be my magnum opus."

*Published in *The Washington Post,* Monday, January 1, 1979, pp. Cl C13. Reprinted with permission of the author and the publisher.

5

THE ILLUSION OF BLACK PROGRESS: A STATEMENT OF THE FACTS*

By

Robert B. Hill
National Urban League

Throughout the 1970's, despite two devastating recessions and record-level unemployment, there has been a continuous flow of pronouncements about the "significant" economic progress of blacks. For example, according to a report by Wattenberg and Scammon, 52 percent of all blacks made it into the middle-class over five years ago.[1] In keepng with the news media's interest in this "surge" in the black middle class, research studies, such as the recent Rand reports, purporting to show a narrowing of the economic gap between blacks and whites have continued to receive an unusual degree of visibility.[2]

As a result of this steady focus on the "new" black middle class, only a small minority of whites now believe that racial discrimination currently exists against blacks. According to two national surveys conducted by Louis Harris & Associates, three-fourths of all whites in 1970 believed that blacks still experienced discrimination in trying to achieve full equality, but by 1977, the proportion of whites who believed that racial discrimination still exists fell to only one-third.[3]

Because of the wide acceptance of the belief in the significant economic progress of blacks, many whites have become increasingly resistent to efforts toward racial equality in the areas of education, employment, housing and economic security. Since they do not believe that significant racial barriers exist, many whites feel that equality of opportunity has already been achieved and there is no need for special emphasis efforts on behalf of blacks and other minorities. On the contrary, increasing numbers of whites are charging "reverse discrimination" and are strongly resisting the use of their tax dollars for social programs on behalf of the poor and minorities. An overriding belief by many persons who voted for passage of Proposition 13 to reduce property taxes in California was that their taxes were going for "unnecessary" social programs that would primarily benefit racial minorities.[4]

However, while it is widely believed that blacks have made strong economic advancement, it is also readily acknowledged that "hard-core" unemployment and poverty still prevail within the black community. But this popular belief in the diminished importance of racial barriers has spawned new terminology for old theories about the persistence of unemployment and poverty among blacks.

The primary reasons given for persistent high unemployment among blacks are "structural" deficiencies, such as *lack* of education, *lack* of job skills, *lack* of work motivation, *lack* of steady employment history, and not such external factors as lack of jobs or racial discrimination. Thus, according to the conventional view, unemployment among blacks remains high primarily because of the influx of "structurally deficient" persons into the labor force, most especially women and teenagers, who would remain jobless even during periods of prosperity and "full" employment.[5]

The facts are different from these assertions.

These are the facts:

1. Contrary to popular belief, the economic gap between blacks and whites is widening. Between 1975 and 1976, the black to white family income ratio fell sharply from 62 to 59 percent.

2. Not only is black unemployment at its highest level today, but the jobless gap between blacks and whites is the widest it has ever been. At the peak of the 1975 recession, the black jobless rate was 1.7 times the white rate, but by the first half of 1978, the black jobless rate was a record 2.3 times higher than the white jobless rate.

3. Employment opportunities have declined sharply for black male heads of families due to the unrelenting recession. Between 1969 and 1976, the proportion of black men heading families who were unemployed or not in the labor force jumped from 18 to 30 percent.

4. The proportion of middle-income black families has not significantly increased. In fact, the proportion of black families with incomes above the Labor Department's intermediate budget level has remained at about one-fourth since 1972.

5. The proportion of upper-income black families has steadily declined. Between 1972 and 1976, the proportion of black families above the government's higher budget level dropped from 12 to 9 percent.

6. The two black societies thesis of a widening cleavage between middle-income and low-income blacks is not supported by national income data. The proportion of black families with incomes under $7,000, as well as those with incomes over $15,000, has remained relatively constant in recent years.

7. The statistical evidence strongly contradicts the popular belief that persistent high unemployment among black youth is primarily due to their educational or skill deficiencies--when job opportunities are greater for white youth with lower educational attainment. White high school dropouts have lower

unemployed rates (22.3%) than black youth with college education (27.2%).

8. Contrary to conventional wisdom, it has been the white labor force, not the black, that has had the largest influx of women and teenagers. Between 1954 and 1977, the proportion of white adult women and teenagers in the total labor force soared from 30 to 41 percent, while the proportion of black adult women and teenagers in the labor force increased from only 5 to 6 percent over that 23-year period.

9. High levels of black unemployment are mainly due to the unavailability of jobs to blacks rather than to their unsuitability for these jobs. And the lack of jobs to blacks is a result of racial discrimination, depressed economy and ineffective targeting.

The persistence of many popular misconceptions about the actual nature and extent of black progress suggests that such terms as "structural" unemployment and "underclass" may become new codewords for "unsolvable" and "intractable" to justify governmental inaction on behalf of racial minorities.

*Excerpts from *The Illusion of Progress, 1978* by Robert B. Hill, Research Director, National Urban League. Reprinted with the permission of the author and the National Urban League Research Department.

REFERENCES TO CHAPTER 5

1. Wattenberg Ben J. and Scammon, Richard M., "Black Progress and Liberal Rhetoric," *Commentary*, April, 1973, pp. 35-44.
2. Smith, James P. and Welch, Finis R., *Race Differences in Earnings: A Survey and New Evidence* and *The Convergence of Racial Equality in Women's Wages*, Santa-Monica, Calif: Rand Corp., 1978.
3. National Urban League, *The State of Black America, 1978*, (Appendix A, Table III-V), New York.
4. Austin, B. William, "White Attitudes Towards Black Discrimination," *The Urban League Review*, 2 (Winter), 1976, pp. 37-42.
5. For example, see Secretary of Labor Marshall's September 1977 Memorandum to the President on "Black Unemployment".

6

THE ECONOMICS OF THE BLACK FAMILY FROM FOUR PERSPECTIVES

By

James A. Hefner
*Morehouse College**

Let us discuss the economic circumstances of the black family from four perspectives: income, economic security, self-determination, and economic freedom. Before proceeding with this discussion, I will first define what I mean by each of these terms (Gregory 1976).

By income I mean the quantity and quality of goods and services consumed and the change in one's wealth-holdings within a specified period of time. This concept transcends that of money income, because it is important to recognize the fact that what one's money can actually purchase is determined by the absolute prices of the goods and services that one consumes. It should be added that the concept of income is concerned not only with those goods provided by private business firms, but with those services provided by government. Furthermore, a change in one's wealth-holdings is important because it determines one's present and future consumption in a period of uncertainty. A wealth-owner can always maintain current consumption should his current source of income falter.

Changes in the economic circumstances of the black family can also be gauged by observing the circumstances that affect its degree of economic security. The economic security of any community, individual, or family is an important source of its well-being. Unemployment and inflation endanger this well-being. The security of an individual is endangered by a loss of income; by those activities that injure health; and in general, by those occurrences that lower the quality of life. More important, the forces that weaken community security overall endanger the security of every family within the community. Programs such as social security, welfare, veterans benefits, and other forms of income maintenance are means of improving economic security, but they do so only if they are administered justly.

The general economic circumstances of the black family can also be evaluated by ascertaining the degree of self-determination enjoyed by members of that household unit within the larger society. Self-determination refers to the extent to which members of a community have influence on those decisions that affect them. In this age of increasing interdependence among nations as well as among individuals, complete control by any community of all of those matters which affect it is impossible. However, some communities and organizations possess greater influence than others. This imbalance can be readily observed in the area of public policy formation, in the access to various types of information, and in the markets of basic industrial goods. When unequal influence exists, self-determination is weakened.

Finally, another criterion for evaluating the economic circumstances of the black family is the degree to which economic freedom exists. In this context, relative freedom is a measure of the ability of individuals to make their own choices about occupation, consumption, and residence without consideration of race, color, sex, or religion.

Now that the perspectives for judgment are clear, I shall examine the overall economic circumstances of the black family. The first point I wish to consider is the influence of income.

INCOME

The income gap between black and white families has widened and is getting larger. The median income of black families rose for a short period of time in the late 1960s to a peak ratio of 62 percent of that of white families in 1976, but has since dropped to its current rate of 57 percent--the lowest in twelve years. The widening of the income gap between black and white families is cause for alarm and should be a priority item for the black community despite the fact that the black median family income, in absolute terms, is at a record high of $9,563.

It should be noted that the black middle class has not increased in proportionate size since 1976. The black middle class has maintained this size since 1976 primarily because of employers' upgrading of blacks in the blue and white collar jobs (especially among craftsmen, professionals and managers), employment gains in high wage industries, increased quality of schooling, greater penetration of blacks into the seniority ranks, and benefits accrued from collective bargaining.

The fact that the proportionate size of the black middle class has remained the same since 1976, while other black families have become worse off economically, has exacerbated an already disturbing problem within the black community. A disturbing feature of the distribution of black income is that the gap between the black under class and the black upper class is widening, and that this gap is even larger than the one separating black families from white families. Unless a significant change is effected, the estrangement between the black ghetto and the black college graduate will worsen (Hefner 1978).

Just as blacks in general do not earn much money, they also lack a sufficient supply of wealth-holdings to fall back on. The grim situation is that white families with annual incomes under $2,500 have, on the average, more net wealth than black families with incomes as high as $14,000 (Terrell 1971). Beyond $14,000 the ratio of black to white wealth falls precipitously. Consider: Black families with incomes between $15,000 and $19,000 have net wealth in the amount of $20,500 as opposed to a net wealth of $43,400 for comparable white families. Black families with incomes over $20,000 have net wealth in the amount of $30,000 compared to $101,000 for white families with the same income. White Americans, on the average, hold roughly 4.5 times as much wealth as black Americans, as compared to 1.5 times as much income (Hefner 1976, pp. 61-62). A disturbing feature of the "wealthlessness" of blacks is that no one group in the black community, including the black middle class, has the resources with which to maintain current consumption should its current source of income falter.

ECONOMIC SECURITY

The economic security of the black family has been devastated by inflation and unemployment. Since black families receive 43 percent less in income than do white families, it stands to reason that black families are even worse off when inflation is considered. For example, between 1976 and 1977, Dr. Robert Hill estimated that the purchasing power of the black family fell by 3 percent due to inflation as compared to an increase of 1 percent in purchasing power for white families. In addition, Dr. Hill found that:

This erosion of black family income relative to whites has occurred in every region of this nation. Between 1975 and 1977, the ratio of black to white family income fell from 67 to 59 percent in the Northeast, from 71 to 62 percent in the Northcentral region, from 67 to 58 percent in the West and from 59 to 57 percent in the South. Although black families still have higher median incomes in the Northeast ($10,285) and Northcentral ($10,690) regions than in the West ($9,285) and South ($8,962), the gap between the incomes of black and white families is becoming more similar among all regions, for the first time (Hill 1979, p. 31).

Even the black middle class has not escaped the erosive effects of inflation. As Dr. Hill puts it:

Unrelenting recession and inflation have also reduced the standard of living for many middle-income black families. In fact, only one-fourth (24 percent of black families) had incomes above $17,106 budget level for 1977 that the U.S. Bureau of Labor Statistics established as an "intermediate" standard of living for American families--which was the same proportion of middle-income black families in 1973. Among whites, however, the proportion of middle-income families increased from 47 to 49 percent between 1976 and 1977--slightly below the 50 percent level among white families in 1973 (Hill 1979, p. 31).

Thus we see the detrimental effect of inflation on the black community. And yet the story does not end here.

First, inflation has led to higher interest rates, which have in turn, cut the rate of housing construction; and blacks are among the worst-housed people in the nation. For a while the housing situation of black families improved considerably. Between 1960 and 1973 the number of blacks who owned their own homes rose to an unprecedented level, and more black homes than ever before had basic plumbing facilities. From 1973 to the present, housing opportunities have receded for blacks, not only because of the higher interest rates that I mentioned earlier, but also because of: sharp reduction in federal funding for housing; increased movement of whites and businesses to suburbia, and the subsequent decline in both employment opportunities for blacks and tax revenue for housing; white opposition to construction of public housing in white areas and opposition to blacks living in suburbs and "better" neighborhoods of cities; tax defaulting and abandonment of urban landlords; and redlining.

Second, inflation has eroded the strength of black institutions, both directly and indirectly. Although these institutions render valuable services to the black community, they have never been, even at the best of times, bastions of financial security. I have in mind institutions of higher learning such as Hampton, Morehouse, Fisk, Spelman, Talladega, Tuskegee, and Atlanta University, which have educated and continue to educate members of black middle class families. I also have in mind institutions such as community development corporations, black-owned businesses, private hospitals, and non-profit agencies.

Finally, inflation further aggravates the already slow rate of wealth (capital) accumulation in the black community. Since it is disadvantageous to be without capital or wealth in a capitalist country, this trend is particularly alarming.

The problem of inflation in the black community is slight compared to that of unemployment. Presently, there are roughly 1.5 million blacks unemployed--a figure which matches the level of joblessness among blacks during the 1975 recession (Hill 1979). Although the black unemployment rate has fallen a little in 1979, it is 2.3 times higher than the rate among whites-- and is the largest it has ever been, according to official indices. However, the story does not end here. Using its own Hidden Unemployment Index, the National Urban League has estimated that the 1979 unemployment rate among blacks is 23 percent as compared to 11 percent among whites (National Urban League 1979).

The implication of the Urban League's estimate of

black unemployment is that the black community is in a depression--not a recession but a depression.

Black unemployment varies significantly by age, sex, education, etc. Among black men the present unemployment rate is roughly 8.9 percent as compared to 3.8 percent among white men. The jobless rate among black women is roughly 12 percent compared to 5 percent among white women. Black teenage unemployment is roughly 40 percent compared to only 14 percent among white teenagers.

The jobless rate among black women and black teenagers deserves additional attention. Because of the high unemployment rate among black women and black teenagers, there has been a reduction in the number of black families with multiple earners while the number of white families with multiple earners has remained roughly the same since 1976. Presently, 55 percent of white families have two or more earners compared to 46 percent of black families (Hill 1979). Since black families in which both husband and wife are employed earn only slightly more than white families in which only the husband works ($12,982 v. $12,381), increased joblessness among black wives compounds the problems of the black family. For it is as true as two and two are four that the black woman's place has never been in the home; she was certainly never placed on a pedestal, or treated as though she were a fragile, delicate creature who received protection. Her role has been that of a toiler at the lowest paying jobs in the nation, but without her there would be a small black middle class. Though less by choice than by circumstance, the black woman is more likely to be single than the white woman. Presently, there are roughly 89 black males to every 100 black females. Add to this black male/black female ratio the joblessness of black males, as well as their low incomes, their greater chance of being incarcerated or on drugs vis-a-vis white males, and the critical problem of the availability of mates for black women stands out clearly (Noble 1975.)

In recent years there has been tension between black males and black females which results from competing for the same jobs and incomes (Noble 1975). They have been joined in the competition by a newcomer--the white female. On the face of it, it would appear that the black man is competing with women, but on a deeper level his real economic competitor, as in other areas of American life, is the white man.

Finally, a word about the black teenage unemployment problem. The grim reality is that roughly a half million black teenagers are always jobless (Anderson 1977). In addition to the obvious fact that many turn to crime and drugs, another fact is that hundreds of black families sink to the depth of poverty because of the lack of support from teenage employment. The teenage unemployment problem is likely to get worse because of the rapid growth of the teenage population and the likelihood of continued recession (at the national level) into 1980.

Growth of employment opportunities alone will not solve the black teenage unemployment problem, because the problem is multi-dimensional. In moments of despair, I sometimes wonder if the intractability of the black youth unemployment problem is so great, particularly considering its unresponsiveness to periods of relative prosperity, that the society in which we live can deal at all with structural unemployment of marginal and stigmatized labor. In moments of optimism, I hold out hope for the resolve of the youth unemployment problem by advocating policy prescriptions. Back-to-school programs should be encouraged. Manpower programs which offer knowledge of career options should be promoted. On-the-job training programs within the private sector should be enhanced. Public service employment should be increased.

Ultimately, the name of the game is to provide young blacks with marketable skills so that they will have options from a life of crime and drugs.

SELF—DETERMINATION

Black self-determination has increased if one accepts political participation as a measure of self-determination. The number of black elected officials has doubled in the last ten years; there are now 120 black mayors, more than 1,000 black council members, roughly 300 black state legislators, 16 black members of the U.S. House of Representatives, and until the fall of 1978, one black senator. Still, blacks constitute only 7/10 of 1 percent of the elected officials in this country; but an interesting question is: Does the increased number of black elected officials suggest potentially greater job opportunities and social programs for members of black families?

The record of the past offers little hope that the cycle of despair and hardship facing black families will reverse. It has not been altered by the Nixon Administration, the Ford Administration, or now the Carter Administration. According to Vernon Jordan of the National Urban League, there is a "creeping malignant growth of a 'new negativism' that calls for weak passive government and indifference to the plight of the poor" (Jordan 1979, p. I).

There is also a malignancy known as the "illusion of inclusion" (Hefner 1976, pp. 257-270). The mere holding of an elected office does not guarantee economic parity for blacks or even movement toward that goal. From the period of 1969 to 1972, the number of black elected officials increased 61 percent, while at the same time the percentage of black income compared to white income decreased from 61 percent to 59 percent. Such evidence indicates that the black political presence has increased only in numbers, not in real policy-making power. Only large increases in black voter registration and voting can be given credit for corresponding increases in black elected officials. The fact remains that the policy-making and decision-making positions have still escaped blacks. Once elected, black officials are still outside the inner sanctum of ultimate policy formation, which is still influenced by those who are producers, wealth owners, and capital generators.

Thus self-determination, like income and economic security, is a very short suit in the black community.

ECONOMIC FREEDOM

At this point, it should be clear to everyone that the black family has limited flexibility to select any pattern of consumption, and that members of black families have limited opportunity to choose any occupation or to reside in any location. Moreover, they are not evaluated without regard to race.

CONCLUSION

We have therefore come full circle. Racism and economics are the societal forces which have the greatest impact on the structure and the functioning of the black family in the United States. To recap the main points:

● We have seen the widening income gap between black and white families, between the black under class and the black middle class.

● We have seen that the economic security of the black family has been devastated by inflation and unemployment, and that the reduction of multiple earners in the black community is likely to exacerbate the gap-widening trend between blacks and whites.

● We have seen that the jobless rate among black

teenagers is staggering, and that the black youth problem is multi-dimensional and indifferent to current
policies designed to be corrective.

● We have seen that the black community has
limited economic freedom, primarily because of
limited self-determination, limited wealth accumulation, and a very tenuous economic security.

While it is true that black advancement will continue to occur among the educated and those from ad-
vantaged backgrounds, it is disturbing that these
blacks may not have the resources with which to maintain current consumption should their current sources
of income falter.

But more education must continue to be emphasized in the black community; not only does it increase the well-being of the black family, but it also
reduces anti-social behavior and the birth-rate as well.
More important, increased education increases wealth
accumulation for blacks far more then it does for
whites.

My objective was to show that the nature of black
oppression in the United States is still very much a
derivative of race, although this point of view is contrary to Sociologist William Wilson's thesis in his new
book, *The Declining Significance of Race*. What must
be observed is the operation of institutional structures
as factors for subordination of blacks. Examples of
what I mean are political entities such as school
boards, zoning boards, and the decision-making
groups in large corporations and in large universities.
The effects of racism are embodied in these institutional structures and distort the bargaining path. The
lack of bargaining power is translated into low relative
economic status for blacks. Because of white allocative
decisions, black Americans have received little benefit
from affirmative action programs, thus creating distur-
bances within the black community itself. Even blacks
who reside in the upper class are the victims of the

allocative decisions of whites, receive less than optimal benefits from the system, and are thus denied. In the present development of America, white racial views provide direction and white economic power determines the magnitude of the economic problems of blacks. White recalcitrance regarding black economic problems is focused in the white decision-making process working through racist-oriented institutional structures. Race is not declining in importance in determining black opportunity and advancement.

REFERENCES

Anderson, Bernard E., "The Youth Unemployment Crisis." Testimony before the House Subcommittee on Employment Opportunities, April, 1977.

Gregory, Karl, "The Black-White Unemployment Differential and Alternatives for Narrowing the Unemployment Gap." Visiting Scholar's Lecture at Morehouse College (memo), 1976. Dr. Gregory's brilliant lecture constitutes the core and vitality of the "four perspectives." The author used his paper most generously. 1976.

Hefner, James A.," The Ghetto." *Public Policy for the Black Community: Strategies and Perspectives.* Edited by M. R. Barnett and J. A. Hefner, New York: Alfred Publishing Co., Inc., 1976.

_____"The Illusion of Inclusion." *Public Policy for the Black Community: Strategies and Perspectives.* New York: Alfred Publishing Co., Inc., 1976.

_____Blacks in the Making of America: An Economic Examination. Convocation Address at Talladega College (memo)., 1978.

Hill, Robert B., "Economic Status of Black Families." *The State of Black America 1979.* New York: National Urban League Publication, 1979

Jordan, Vernon E., "Introduction." *The State of Black America 1979.* New York: National Urban League Publication, 1979.

Noble, Jeanne, "Status of the Black American Woman," *World Encyclopedia of Black Peoples,* Volume 1 Conspectus. Michigan: Scholarly Press, Inc., 1975.

Terrell, Henry S., "Wealth Accumulation of Black and White Families: The Empirical Evidence." *Journal of Finance,* May, 1971.

Dr. Hefner is Charles E. Merrill Professor of Economics, Morehouse College, Atlanta, Georgia. In 1979, he was a Visiting Research Associate, Department of Economics, Harvard University.

7

UNDERCLASS: AN APPRAISAL*

By

Dorothy K. Newman, Lecturer and Consultant

MEANING

The Declining Significance of Race by William J. Wilson is about "class" as much as race, with substantial emphasis on the underclass. The underclass discussed is almost without exception black. The definition of "class" has high priority, and appears on the first page of the preface. This is proper, since "class" is truly, as the author writes, "a slippery concept." The definition is precise:

"...in this study the concept (class) means any group of people who have more or less similar goods, services, or skills to offer for income in a given economic order and who therefore receive similar financial remuneration in the marketplace."

Under that meaning those deemed especially qualified in the marketplace will be affluent and upper class, and those deemed least qualified will be poor and

---

*This paper was greatly improved as a result of careful reading and insightful critique by Dr. Barbara L. Carter, Associate Vice President of the University of the District of Columbia. The author is responsible for whatever faults remain. The author was formerly associated with the U.S. Labor Department and the National Urban League.

therefore lower class. Even without explicit guidance the reader concludes correctly that the concept of underclass derives from the definition of class. The underclass are the poor. This fits in with the book's definition of the black underclass at one point,** as those who are below the officially designated low-income level.

The quoted definition of class could exclude those not in the labor force or marketplace, which, of course, was not the author's intent. The reader quickly realizes that the definition necessarily incorporates children and other dependents within the class of their respective household breadwinners or income recipients.

The definition assigning the underclass to the lower class is Webster's definition too, in the New Collegiate Dictionary, where "underclass" is "lower class." If readers have in mind a definition of the prefix "under" "denoting inferiority in rank or importance," as found in the Oxford Universal Dictionary's third edition, the word "inferiority" should be construed only as an inferior position in rank order. It is a matter of placement or location, not of worth.

POINT COUNTERPOINT

Not counting the mid 1970's deep recession, the black underclass has remained close to 7.5 million between 1970 and 1977,* but slid two percentage points, from 33.5 to 31.3 percent of the black population. The white underclass fell by one million (from 17.5 to 16.4

**Page 181, footnote 22 to Chapter 6.

*The snail's pace at which hard data are collected and analyzed leaves us always in the awkward position of presenting the past and predicting the present. The most recent factual details now available about income, low income, or the underclass are for 1977, although we are writing in 1979.

million), and declined slightly from 10 to 9 percent of
the white population. While the proportion of underclass blacks far exceeds the proportion of underclass
whites, the chance of meeting, interviewing, sitting or
living next to, or working with an underclass white person is double the chance of having the same contact
with an underclass black. The white underclass includes half again as many children under 18 as the
black underclass did in 1977 (6 million compared with
4 million), twice as many 18 to 21 year olds just entering the job market, and almost two and a half times as
many 22 to 24 year olds. The white underclass also had
two and a half times as many as the black underclass in
the prime working years, whether one thinks of this
group as 25 to 44 years old, or 25 to 54.

The black underclass does not even match the
white underclass in the central cities of metropolitan
areas where they were half a million fewer in 1977--4.3
million black compared with 4.8 million white.

Only within the officially designated low-income
or poverty areas of metropolitan areas does the black
underclass exceed the white--2.8 million compared
with 1.3 million. This is by no means the majority of
both groups of the underclass— 36 percent of the black
underclass and 8 percent of the white. Only black
neighborhoods are currently called ghettos, and blacks
are more likely to live in low-income areas than whites,
regardless of whether or not they are low income.
White underclass persons in the poverty areas of
metropolitan central cities are not usually referred to
today as living in a ghetto, unless the neighborhood
they occupy is predominantly black.

ECONOMIC DISTANCE BETWEEN CLASSES

Most economic measures are crude in the extreme
because they exclude assets that can be converted to in-

come, assets which, in many cases are income producing besides being convertible into sizeable amounts of cash. Because blacks have much less of this wealth, the economic distance between underclass blacks and middle and upper class blacks does not begin to compare with the ranges in the white majority. The white underclass, which is on a level with the black underclass, is light years away from the white wealthy-- its Rockefellers, Morgans, and Geneens. But the black underclass is but a stone's throw from its middle class in our still segregated society, and not much farther, either in distance or riches, from its wealthy. Few black families are truly rich in the traditional sense.

The median income of black families was well within the $9,000 to $10,000 range between 1970 and 1977;** half had less and half had more. Fewer than 10 percent were comfortably middle class or well off with $25,000 or more during the period; 25 percent had less than $5,000 (all in constant 1977 dollars). This leaves little room or few dollars within which to attribute any substantial growth in a gap between the black underclass and the black middle or upper class. A widening gap might be ascribed or perceived, but with the use of a noneconomic definition of class.

In contrast with the black underclass, the white underclass is much farther removed from its middle and upper class, and growing farther apart. White median income was $16,000 to $17,000 in the 1970-77 period, and there was an increasing 19 to 24 percent in the $25,000 and over income group. Black families who are comfortably middle to well off increased too, from 7 to 9 percent from 1970 to 1977. The fragility of this modest gain and small proportion at the top becomes ever more clear today as the tide turns "Bakke-wards,"* protesting affirmative action for

---

*Taken from the title "The Weber Case: Another step Bakke-wards," article by Herman Schwartz in the May 29, 1979 issue of *The Nation*.
**In constant 1977dollars.

blacks on all fronts. Benign neglect of the early 1970s has become confrontation in the late 1970s. The proliferation of contenders for affirmative action could be affecting all black earners.

THE UNDERCLASS AND THE ECONOMY

The persistence of stagflation, which has eroded employment prospects and buying power generally could be hurting everyone. The underclass as a whole could be increasing. For one thing, it is competing with several million workers recruited, trained, and employed by American corporations which have established plants overseas in such places as Taiwan, Hong Kong, Greece, Turkey, and Chile.

This overseas U.S. corporate labor force has less schooling and skills than America's underclass. Yet overseas workers are qualified for learning most jobs in American industry, just as most Americans are. Increasing technology continues to make jobs easier, not harder. Skill formerly required of workers themselves are now built into machines throughout industry, from hospitals, banks, and stores to the most technologically advanced manufacturing plants. Need is growing for the less trained, and shrinking for the highly technical or professional.

Employers still demand formal education here in the U.S., and even advanced degrees when such credentials are not necessary to do the work. Thus, it is conceivable that overqualified and educated people are now, or soon will be doing many of the underclass jobs of today, but at higher pay.

In terms of jobs, a shift occurred chiefly among the black underclass between 1970 and 1977 away from laboring and service jobs into clerical and sales work. In contrast, little change took place in the occupational distribution of the American labor force as a whole in the 1970s or among the white underclass. A

large and similar percentage of white and black
underclass workers were in stores, offices, and industry
in 1977--43 and 45 percent.

These were the employed. Some of the reason for
low income is unemployment itself, and not what the
job is and what it pays. Unemployment rates were
higher in 1977 than in 1970--7.0 compared with 4.9.
The underclass suffered disproportionately, but the
black group much more than the white, so that the two
rates diverged over the years. The unemployment rates
of the black and white underclass in 1970, though
high, were relatively close (12.5 vs. 10.2). The disparity
was substantial by 1977 (25.6 for the black underclass
compared with 15.6 for the white). This disparity is
puzzling. Remembering that the marketplace employs
and trains illiterate workers abroad to produce
American goods, it is illogical to conclude that the
black underclass is less employable than they, or than
the white American underclass, unless "white" is included in the "goods, services, and skills" being offered
in the marketplace.

REFERENCES

Barnet, Richard J. and Ronald E. Muller, *Global Reach.* New
York, Simon and Schuster, 1974.

Newman, Dorothy K. and Nancy J. Amidei, Barbara L. Carter,
Dawn Day, William J. Kruvant, and Jack S. Russell. *Protest,
Politics, and Prosperity: Black Americans and White Institutions,
1940-75.* New York, Pantheon Books, 1978. Especially Chapters
2, 3, and 7.
U. S. Bureau of the Census, Current Population Reports, *Con-
sumer Income.* Series p-60. No. 81, Table 19; No. 86, Table 4;
No. 91, Table 4; No. 98, Table 4; No. 102, Table 4; No. 118,
Table 12; No. 119, Tables 5 and 30.

8

CAMOUFLAGING THE COLOR LINE: A CRITIQUE*

By

Harry Edwards, University of California, Berkeley

A review prepared for *Social Forces*, April, 1979, of *The Declining Significance of Race* by William Julius Wilson.

William Wilson's latest book demonstrates once again the value of calculated, evocative packaging and promotion--or, in marketing lingo, *"hype"*--in advancing a product that otherwise might generate far less than extraordinary attention, much less opportunistic commendation. Under cover of a highly provocative and controversial title, the author presents a basically mediocre work that is both incredibly tendentious and critically deficient empirically and theoretically. All too often, not only does he fail to persuasively substantiate his contentions, but many of his inferences and conclusions are so discrepant relative to "supportive" evidence that the former are reduced to non-sequiturs. And most unfortunately, the author is apparently quite content to summarily dismiss troublesome potential and *existing* structural and sociopolitical developments threatening the fundamental credibility of his central thesis, i.e., that in America's modern industrial era, economic class position, *not race,* has emerged as the major determinant of Black life chances. The validity of his contention hinges upon the viability of a series of explicitly stipulated circumstances whose presumed integrity has been highly questionable for some years now, and which, further, show every sign of accelerated deterioration.

The following constitute the critically imperative foundations of Wilson's argument:

1.   The existence of *expanding* high-wage, high-status job opportunities in both the corporate and government sectors (pp. 88, 97-104, 109-111, 120-121, 150-154).

2.   The forceful intervention of the state to remove contemporary racist obstacles and to rectify the historical legacy of artificially discriminatory barriers to employment opportunities through court action, occupational rights legislation and executive orders (such as Executive Order 11246 which mandated Affirmative Action programs); (p. 150).

3.   The existence of a powerful political and social movement against job discrimination (pp. 134-141, 153).

4.   The existence of stable if not expanding access by minorities to higher education and advanced technological training opportunities (pp. 18-121).

Any substantial deterioration in the optimal character of any one of these critical circumstances would seriously impune the integrity of the author's analysis *by his own admission.* Nevertheless, he fails to even cite--much less systematically address--widely published and acknowledged evidence to the effect that *all four* circumstances have deteriorated significantly; and his cavalier response to a purely suppositious question regarding the deterioration of circumstance (1) above is that "...although it is possible that an economic disaster could produce racial com-

petition for higher paying jobs and White efforts to exclude talented Blacks, it is difficult to entertain this
idea as a real possibility *in the face of the powerful
political and social movement against job discrimination...there is little available evidence to suggest that
the economic gains of privileged Blacks will be revers-
ed...*" (p. 153, emphasis added).

Such "non-responses" unavoidably reflect upon
the level of veracity, naivete or both exhibited in the
book, especially given the contextual genesis and implications of such structural and sociopolitical
phenomena as the Bakke and Weber cases; the
precipitous decline in Black college enrollment as well
as Black faculty and staff recruitment since 1971; the
scores of individual and class-action assaults by Whites
against Affirmative Action programs; the increasing
neglect of both affirmative action compliance and en-
forcement nationwide--particularly as these apply to
high-wage, high-status job positions; the passage of
"Proposition 13" in California and the increasing signs
of a growing "tax revolt" nationally; "stagflation;" and
the energy crisis--just to cite a few well-known and
highly documented mitigating considerations. These
factors have already contributed toward not only
halting but *reversing* economic gains at all levels of
Black society--particularly those accruing to the Black
middle class. Indeed, according to both this book and
one of Wilson's earlier works, the mere *potential* com-
petitiveness of minorities in an economic environment
characterized by *declining expectations* (not to speak
of actual deterioration) has historically been sufficient
to generate a shift from inter-individual to inter-racial
competition and even conflict--particularly over
scarce, highly valued rewards.

The credibility of the work is also vulnerable on
other grounds. Far too frequently the author posits
conclusions and inferences that are substantially
idiosyncratic or simply irrelevant to "supporting" data.

For example, I find the empirical data presented in the second paragraph, page 114, far too general and unfocused to corroborate his contention that a "rapid rise in the proportion of 'high-cost' disadvantaged students" corresponded to a "drop in overall educational performance in urban public schools." Even more disturbing is the inclusion of utterly superfluous statistics on remedial help required by "half the entering freshmen" at City University of New York following open enrollment.

Similarly, Wilson's conclusions regarding some broad historical analyses leave much to be desired. For instance, conclusions derived from the historical analysis of Black-White relations in the pre-industrial, antebellum South fail to encompass the demonstrable possibility that elite slave-owning Whites and non-slave owning Whites arrived at mutually accommodative economic arrangements--largely at the expense of Blacks. Inadequate also is his treatment of Black-White relations during the period following the Civil War and before World War II (see Chapters 1-4). While such a track neatly camouflages inadequacies in his analysis, it speaks very poorly for the credibility of the work.

And apparently it is not simply the complex, broad historical concerns that confounded the author's analytical astuteness. On page 24, he resolutely asserts that "...the ownership of slaves was a privilege enjoyed by only a small percentage of free families in the South. *Of the 1,156,000 free southern families in 1860, only 385,000 (roughly one-fourth) owned slaves...*" (emphasis added). His insistence that "roughly" only one-fourth of the free families owned slaves is reiterated on page 45. While his assertion ostensibly supports his claims that slaveowners' political hegemony was based on the structure of the economic system and not upon their proportionate numbers, it also brutalizes elementary mathematical logic. For if 385,000 approximates some "rough" fraction of 1,156,000, it is *one-third*, not *one-fourth*. Given the fact that the author contends (on page 56) that one-third Blacks in major cities constitutes a population sufficient to "raise the specter" of Black control of cities (even with *no* discernible economic base, pages 111-117), his argument that the economic structure alone was responsible for slaveowner hegemony is severely undermined--even assuming that there was hegemony rather than White slaveowner and non-slaveowner mutual accommodation at Black expense.

Space limitation will allow for mention of only one other seriously erroneous contention typical of other instances throughout the book. The author's assertion (page 135) that "Lower-class Blacks had little involvement in civil rights politics up to the mid-1960's" is almost too ludicrous to comment upon. The statement seriously demeans the contributions of the thousands of domestics, "bus boys," unemployed and under-employed Blacks who participated (along with middle-class Blacks and sympathetic Whites)--often times at great personal risk--in bus boycotts, voter registration drives, school desegregation efforts and countless other non-violent direct action protests throughout the 1950's and 1960's. Again, the statement serves the author's contention that "...Black protest tends often to be a by-product of economic class position..." as opposed to over-riding racial group circumstances, but it also flys in the face of *documented* historical fact.

Overall, the book should be recommended owing to the character and sheer volume of its limitations rather than for reasons related to any contributions it purports to make. For those seriously interested in the subject matter covered, however, I would strongly suggest consideration of the Carnegie funded study *Protest, Politics and Prosperity: Black Americans and White Institutions,* by Dorothy K. Newman, et al. New York: Pantheon, 1978. Upon any objective appraisal of the evidence and findings presented in this book, as well as others too numerous to cite, one of two conclusions becomes inevitable: 1) far from declining, the significance of race in the life chances of minorities in America is increasing at an accelerating rate; or 2) if the significance of race has declined it has done so only for working- and middle-class *Whites* owing to their increasing "niggerization" within the context of *their* intraracial class struggles. Paradoxically the latter alternative results no less in the maintenance, if not an increase, in the significance of race for minorities since they are thrown into greater competition with downwardly mobile Whites.

In sum, then, Wilson's work not withstanding, the validity of Dr. DuBois' prophetic observation remains utterly unchallenged: the overwhelmingly significant problem of America in the twentieth century remains *"the problem of the color line."*

9

IF WE WON, WHY AREN'T
WE SMILING?*

By

Richard Margolis, Literary Editor of Change Magazine
*A review for Change, April, 1979 of The Declining Significance of Race: Blacks
and Changing American Institutions by William Julius Wilson, University of
Chicago and Protest, Politics, and Prosperity: Black Americans and White Institutions, 1940-75 by Dorothy K. Newman, et al. New York: Pantheon.*

The near-ubiquity of white racism in America has
long been an open secret, but not until relatively recent
times has it been widely perceived as a social problem.
Chief Justice Roger Brooke Taney in his now notorious
Dred Scott decision (1857) doubtless spoke for the most
white citizens of his day when without a trace of bad
conscience he approvingly thumbnailed the history of
American racism. "For more than a century before the
Declaration of Independence," the Chief Justice noted,
"the Negroes had been regarded as beings of an inferior order...so far inferior that they had no rights
which a white man was bound to respect." In those
times of moral certitude, and for generations to come,
the notion of "Negro inferiority" was not so much an
issue as it was an axiom. Journalists diligently reported
it; commentators soberly confirmed it; scholars
ponderously "proved" it. So embedded in the national
psyche was white hubris that the pop historian Hendrik

Van Loon, in a 1923 award-winning essay on "Tolerance," could casually observe that "a Zulu riding in a Rolls Royce is still a Zulu." (Uncle Remus back then professed a larger vision: "Niggers is niggers now, but de time wuz w'en we 'uz all niggers tergedder.")

Very likely it wasn't until the 1930s that people in any large numbers began to see something ugly in all that arrogance, and to suspect that the white emperor wore no clothes. For many, Gunnar Myrdal made the new consciousness official with his opening lines to *An American Dilemma* (1944): "There is a 'Negro problem' in the United States," he wrote, "and most Americans are aware of it...Americans have to react to it, politically as citizens and...privately as neighbors." As Myrdal and his coauthors made clear in that large and seminal work, the "Negro problem" was really a white problem; for they demonstrated beyond cavil the extent to which we had institutionalized racial discrimination, weaving it tightly-perhaps inextricably-into the fabric of our national life. This we did in defiance of what Myrdal called "the American Creed," by which he meant that shared set of beliefs roughly embodied in the first phrases of the Declaration of Independence. It was his opinion that the resulting clash between the ideal of equality and the ideology of racism had made a battleground of our collective conscience. "America," he wrote, "is continuously struggling for its soul."

So--how now goes the struggle? From the two books at hand we get two different answers, as well as two different temperatures of scholarship. William Julius Wilson, a black sociologist at the University of Chicago, is cool, theoretical, and dispassionate in tone. Using history as his guide and various economic theories as his goal, Wilson attempts to persuade us that the very boundaries of the struggle have lately shifted, and that Myrdal's "Negro problem" is now largely extinct; what we have instead is a class problem, wherein a sizable and enduring black underclass finds itself the victim, not of racist tradition, but of technological progress. That this youthful army of the unemployed happens to be black, says Wilson, is "an accident of history" rather than a consequence of continuing white discrimination.

Dorothy K. Newman is also a sociologist, one who spent years plumbing the empirical depths of segregation as research director of the National Urban League. Compared with Wilson, Newman and her author-colleagues are hot, pragmatic, and compassionate. While their book, billed as a 35-year update of Myrdal, perfunctorily affirms the gains blacks have made since the early sixties, it concentrates more on the gains they have not made, citing time and again "the resistance of white Americans to accepting blacks as equals." The message is that white racism remains alive and well, and that the American soul struggle is still up for grabs.

Both these books have been out long enough now to have attracted their partisans and their reprovers; and if my periodical readings are a fair sample, it seems clear that in the war of reviews Wilson has won hands down. Even the *New York Times,* not the world's most roseate journal, considered Wilson's sophisticated optimism more convincing than Newman's straight-forward gloom. Yet Newman, for all her old-fashioned, civil-righter's biases, surely has a firmer grip on current racial realities than does Wilson. (Here I should mention a "conflict of interest": I was lucky enough to read an early draft of the Newman manuscript and to make some minor suggestions).

If most reviewers have preferred Wilson's bright mirage to Newman's dark mirror, it may be because they, like the rest of us, are weary of domestic strife and of guilt-edged sermons. Many Americans these days are understandably eager to accept glad racial tidings with no questions asked, especially when they come to us courtesy of a brilliant black scholar with a taste for abstractions. Pangloss, it turns out, is a master theoretician.

In *The Declining Significance of Race,* Wilson ranges freely and facinatingly over the history of racial oppression in the United States—from pre-Civil War days, when the estates of white southern aristocrats were irrigated by the sweat of black slaves, to pre-New Deal days, when northern industrialists and their white workers frequently combined to shut blacks out of the job market. (Except during strikes: Wilson includes a startling table showing the extent to which corporations, between 1916 and 1934, relied on scab black labor to bust lily-white unions).

His history is largely economic; although he says he does not subscribe to "the view that racial problems are necessarily derived from more fundamental class problems," he has nonetheless made a central issue of the constantly shifting job market, persuasively linking the course of racism to the aspirations of white capitalists and to the fears of white workers. No one has done this better or more tellingly. Wilson is able to establish, for example, that the late nineteenth century was for the North "an unprecedented period of racial unity and integration," distinguished by relatively equal employment opportunities and by the passage in several states of civil rights legislation. Only later, when southern blacks began to drift northward in large numbers, did frightened whites repeal the laws and lock the factory gates.

Old patterns of economic discrimination, says Wilson, began to break up with the New Deal, when the more liberal unions lowered the color bar a notch or two. The production demands of World War II, followed by two decades of nearly uninterrupted prosperity, further eroded Jim Crowism in the North. Finally, the protests and civil rights reforms of the six-

ties completed the progressive cycle begun almost half
a century ago, and brought us, in Wilson's view, to our
present nonracial impasse.

He devotes considerable space in support of his
proposition that there are now two classes of black
Americans—the uneducated poor and the educated affluent—where before there had been only one (all
poor). Middle-class blacks, he argues, are doing just
fine, thanks to the new, nondiscriminatory job market;
lower-class blacks, meanwhile, suffer hardships that
are largely unrelated to race. These ghetto dwellers,
says Wilson, simply have had the ill luck to have come
to age at the wrong moment—when the economy is
slowing down, when factories are automating, and
when corporations are moving outward from cities to
suburbs. Therefore, "It would be nearly impossible to
comprehend the economic plight of lower-class blacks
in the inner city by focusing solely on racial oppression;
that is, [on] the overt and explicit effort of whites to
keep blacks in a subjugated state...."

And: "It would also be difficult to explain the
rapid economic improvement of the black elite by
rigidly postulating the view that traditional patterns of
discrimination are still salient in the labor-market
practices of American industries." After which Wilson
nails down his main plank: "Economic class is now a
more important factor than race in determining job
placement for blacks."

Wilson's news has been so cheerfully received
because what he seems to be telling us is precisely what
we've always longed to hear: that we have managed to
slip through the horns of our American Dilemma and
that the ancient battle for racial justice is nearly won.
But, then, why aren't we dancing in the streets? Is it
possible that the report of racism's death has been
greatly exaggerated?

Newman's *Protest, Politics, and Prosperity* is
helpful here. It pitilessly documents our sins and, by

coincidence, spotlights some missing beams in Wilson's logical structure. Take the matter of employment, which Newman, like Wilson, thinks central to any discussion of race. In Newman's book, today's labor market for blacks is still no Promised Land; it remains a white-dominated wilderness, full of prickly prejudices and discriminatory practices. "The black struggle for jobs continues," Newman notes, "because inequality still prevails. Racial discrimination and acceptance of the resulting inequality remain embedded in the white-dominated job market, buttressed by many rationalizations." An accompanying chart bears her out. It compares the rise, from 1940-75, of black occupational positions with those of white workers. True, blacks rose faster than did whites, but as of 1975 blacks had not even reached the whites' 1940 level! Thus what Wilson would call progress Newman has labeled disaster.

This book is especially persuasive in two other areas—education and housing. Where Wilson treats these subjects mechanistically, citing inferior schools and neighborhoods as two more nonracial reasons blacks can't get jobs, Newman confronts them squarely as racial issues. She observes first that corporations often use such social ills as excuses for continuing racist employment policies, and second that segregated housing, far from being an economic accident, is part of a broad social intent on the part of white-controlled institutions, including the banks, the real estate industry, and some government agencies.

In a chapter on "Learning Without Earning," Newman points to industry's new, credential-ridden job standards, which compel prospective employees to seek college degrees in order to "learn" how to perform tasks that in the past have been adequately handled by persons who never finished high school; and she suggests tht such credentialism is really a smoke screen for racism—a respectable devise allowing corporations to

shun blacks without seeming to violate the tenets of affirmative action. Perhaps she carries the point too far;
still, her approach is refreshingly tough-minded in contrast to Wilson's easy acceptance of corporate ra-
tionales.

Likewise, in a chapter called "But Not Next
Door," Newman and her coauthors are able to
demonstrate that housing is "one of the areas of
greatest white resistance to integration," that since
1960 neighborhood segregation has grown worse, and
that federal policy has been of little or no use in loosen-
ing the suburban noose that chokes the black inner city. Newman correctly suggests that polite, white,
suburban racism—pampered by zoning exclusions and
financed by the taxes of newly located industries—comes very close to the heart of the employment problem. As Patricia Harris, Secretary of the
Department of Housing and Urban Development, has
observed, "Communities that say we will take the
benefit of a good tax base but will not let people who
might benefit from that employment live in this community ought to be required to think about the injustice of that."

Ultimately, for all its strengths, the Wilson book
works to postpone that elusive moment of truth for
white Americans, while the Newman book tries to keep
us struggling toward the light. It appears we have miles
to go before our soul awakes.

*Reprinted with permission from *Change* Magazine, Volume II, No. 3 (April
1979). Copyrighted by the Council on Learning, New Rochelle, New York 10801.

10

THE CHANGING--NOT DECLINING--SIGNIFICANCE OF RACE*

By

Thomas F. Pettigrew, Harvard University

A review for *Contemporary Sociology* of *The Declining Significance of Race: Blacks and Changing American Institutions,* by William Julius Wilson.

From an emphasis on racism in his previous work, William Wilson now asserts the paramount significance of social class. Three facets of this volume must be considered in order to judge his new position: (1) its analysis of black-white relations throughout American history; (2) its intimations of a theoretical alternative to "orthodox Marxist" and split labor-market theory; and (3) its conclusion that the significance of race is declining.

(1) Wilson divides American race relations into three historical stages - *the preindustrial* ("the period of *plantation economy and racial-caste oppression"* extending to the Civil War), *the industrial* ("the period of *industrial expansion, class conflict, and racial oppression"* extending from the Civil War to the New Deal), and *the modern industrial* ("the period of *progressive transition from racial...to class inequalities"* extending

---

*Reprinted with permission of the author, *Contemporary Sociology,* and the American Sociological Association.

from World War II to the present). The book then attempts to demonstrate that each stage's unique form of racial interaction was shaped by its distinctive economy and polity.

Such a thesis is hardly ground-breaking. The paternalistic versus competitive modes of the preindustrial and industrial stages follow closely Pierre van den Berghe's well-known dichotomy. And particular secondary sources are relied upon heavily for the descriptions of each stage, especially the writings on slavery of Eugene Genovese, on southern history of Vann Woodward, and on black politics of Ira Katznelson and Martin Kilson. Since *The Declining Significance of Race* is barely 50,000 words with considerable repetition, the historical review is necessarily highly selective and a bit superficial at points. For example, it is repeatedly asserted that the South's white lower class alone legalized Jim Crow segregation at the turn of the century (pp. 17, 56-57, 146). This statement fits Wilson's simplified scheme of economic determinism, but it ignores the mixed evidence presented by sociological and historical sources. In some states, such as Virginia, the elite was largely responsible, and in others it was highly implicated.

Nonetheless, Wilson's review presents a brief overview of American racial history that is provocative and engaging if not novel and definitive. But its purpose is more ambitious, for it is proposing a new theoretical perspective.

(2) The author outlines two major economic class theories of race relations. "Orthodox Marxists" are said to view racial conflict as a "mask for privilege" that conceals the capitalists' efforts to divide workers and exploit minorities. Oliver Cox, Paul Sweezy, and Michael Reich are among those so categorized. Edna Bonacich's split labor-market theory is cited in opposition to the Marxist position. Instead of associating racial stratification with capitalist manipulations,

Bonacich associates it with the higher-paid, white working class that endeavors to exclude the lower-paid, black working class. Wilson then tests these rival predictions in his historical descriptions.

Some eras are regarded as consistent with Marxist contentions — slavery in the antebellum South and the short-lived Black Codes immediately following the Civil War. Others appear consistent with split labor-market ideas — racial stratification in the late antebellum North and the postbellum South. But neither theory, Wilson contends, can account for all of these key eras, nor are they relevant to the present, modern industrial stage. They fail because they do not focus on the constraints imposed by the particular systems of production in each region and period. And they shed little light on the present period, because they do not focus sufficiently on the polity.

One criticism of this argument is that it attacks incomplete forms of these class theories. Marxists *have* provided explanations for the rise of Jim Crow. Wilson may not find such explanations persuasive, but his abbreviated discussion does not consider them.

A deeper criticism, however, is the book's failure to define an alternative. It is interesting to argue the central importance of particular systems of production; but, without an explicit general statement tying this argument together with testable predictions, there is no theory being offered. Wilson realizes this weakness, for he writes in a footnote:

Of course, for our purposes, it would be desirable to develop a more comprehensive theory that systematically integrates propositions concerning the roles of the system of production with propositions drawn from the economic class theories. Although I do not attempt such an ambitious project in this book, I do believe that my theoretical arguments have sufficient scope to deal with a variety of historical situations and constitute at least an implicit theory of social change and race relations. (Pp. 164-165).

But it is precisely this "ambitious project" that would have made the work a major contribution. This recalls the same problem with Wilsons earlier volume. *Power, Racism and Privilege* (New York: MacMillan, 1973) was also a mini-sized descriptive volume that never stated the argument in explicit, testable, theoretical terms. My review of that book (*Social Forces*, 1975, *54*, 291-292) closed with a paragraph that equally well fits this one:

In short, this book represents an interesting initial statement and outline of a broad theoretical approach... It needs further specification to be a full-blown theory. One hopes this elaboration will appear in later works by the author. (P. 292)

(3) But, as its attention-provoking title suggests, *The Declining Significance of Race* departs from the earlier work in its conclusion. He maintains that "class has become more important than race in determining black life-chances in the modern industrial period." (P. 150) A segmented labor market leads to shrinking opportunities for poorly trained blacks and "unprecedented job opportunities in the growing government and corporate sectors" for well-trained blacks. And, Wilson reasons, the increasing importance of class must signify the decreasing importance of race.

The rapidly increasing stratification within the black world has long been recognized. President Lyndon Johnson made this phenomenon the basis of his famous 1965 Howard University address. The point was formalized by the economist, Andrew Brimmer, in the 1966 edition of *The American Negro Reference Book* edited by John Davis (Englewood Cliffs, N.J.: Prentice-Hall, 1966). Brimmer, later a Governor of the Federal Reserve Board, showed that income was increasingly more maldistributed among non-white than white families. Neither these early uses nor later economic critiques of the idea are cited by Wilson, though reference is made to two later unpublished papers on the subject by Brimmer.

What *is* new, however, is the notion that this increasing stratification within black America somehow necessarily signals the declining significance of race. None of the many writers who have drawn attention to this phenomenon ever advanced this conclusion. Certainly, these observers viewed the growing variance as indicating the *changing* significance of race. But neither the phenomenon itself, nor the data cited by Wilson, reveal any decline in the importance of race as such. Indeed, only two of the book's 15 tables are relevant, for they combine class and race effects on unemployment (Table 11) and on parental presence with own children (Table 15). These tables show strong main effects for both the class and race variables, moderate interactions, and no evidence of "the declining significance of race" whatsoever.

The fallacy seems to lie in the belief that an increase in the predictive power of one set of variables (class) necessitates a decrease in the predictive power of another set (race). Others interpret these same data to mean that, while social class as a main effect *is* increasing for economic outcomes, the class and race interaction terms are also increasing and race as an important main effect persists. Thus, the black poor are far worse off than the white poor, and the black middle-class still has a long way to catch up with the white middle-class in wealth and economic security. Black median family income is not closing the gap with white median family income even with the growing disparity within black America.

To be sure, Wilson hedges on his conclusion. He admits that it applies only to the economic sphere. He knows that white resistance continues to rage against residential integration, public school desegregation, and black control of central cities — all signs of *"the unyielding importance of race* in America" (p. 152, italics added). But these "antagonisms," he insists, are far less historically and individually crucial for access to opportunities than economic antagonism. This counter assumes relative independence of economics from the "socio-political" sectors of life — an unwarranted assumption in the light of the sociological literature generally and the racial discrimination literature in particular. Wilson himself implies these connections when he stresses the economic consequences of the current concentration of blacks in declining core cities.

Therefore, I believe that the chief conclusion of this volume — *The Declining Significance of Race* — to be premature at best, dangerously wrong at worst. The unqualified title attracts attention to the book. But it unwittingly risks adding unsubstantiated support to the dominant ideological myth of the current "post-Reconstruction" phase of American race relations: namely, that racial problems were basically solved during the 1960s, and thus there is no continuing need for such measures as affirmative action and metropolitan approaches to public school desegregation. In fairness, Wilson does not make such arguments; in fact, I am certain that he would repudiate them forcefully. But in the politically charged arena of race relations, his misleading title has already been exploited by conservative spokesmen.

Preferable to the present volume, then, would have been a book entitled "The *Changing* Significance of Race" that spelled out the author's theoretical ideas in detail.

11

ON THE DECLINING—AND INCREASING—SIGNIFICANCE OF RACE

By

Charles Payne, Williams College

The reaction to William Wilson's *Declining Significance of Race* may tell us more about the state of the sociological art and about the state of American race relations than will the book itself. Hailed in some quarters as a signal contribution to the literature, the work is being blasted elsewhere with the charge that it is thoroughly distorting in content and probably reactionary in its consequences. That the reactions themselves seem motivated partly by racial considerations is more than mildly ironic.

We may think of Wilson as developing two interlocked, but distinguishable arguments. There is a general theory which divides American racial history into three stages and argues that the patterns of racial conflict and dominance in each period are shaped by changing conditions in the economy and polity. This is in distinction to those theories giving primacy to one or the other. There is also a special theory which applies the principles of the general theory to the modern era

117

in such a way as to lead to the conclusion that the significance of race is declining, an unhappy phrase by which Wilson apparently means something like this: the extent to which whites self-consciously and overtly use race as a means to suppress Black life-chances, as measured by income and occupational distribution, has declined, while the significance of social class background among Blacks for the same outcomes has increased to a point where it is now more important than race.

Although it takes some interesting side-trips, the main business in the earlier part of the work seems to be the attempt to understand the economic basis for nineteenth century racism, which comes to mean an attempt at assessing the relative value of the orthodox Marxist and the split-labor interpretations of the question. By the first -- and labeling anything "orthodox Marxist" is certain to fuel an argument -- Wilson refers to the position that racism is directly attributable to the profit-motivated manipulations of an economic elite. On the other hand, the split-labor approach (Bonacich: 1972, 1976) traces racism to the attempts of a relatively well-paid and economically powerful segment of the working class to protect its position against the threat posed by the existence of cheaper labor pools. Both of these are materialist theories, of course. Aside from a short discussion of racial belief systems which raises some pointed questions about the conventional interpretation of the influence of industrialization on race relations, Wilson is primarily concerned with determining what type of materialist theory best fits that part of our history, giving just slight attention to non-materialist possibilities.

From the antebellum period until some point shortly after the Civil War, Wilson takes the system of production as his dominant factor. The simplicity of the division of labor made white workers marginal, insuring the economic hegemony of the slave-holding aristocracy which they were able to translate into political hegemony as well. Race relations under these circumstances developed a paternalistic quality, i.e., they involved specification of reciprocal duties and rights. Wilson is careful about distinguishing his position from the more extreme treatments of paternalism -- classically Elkins (1959) -- which focus on the presumed tendency of slaves to internalize the system's norms. It is the period that Wilson finds the clearest evidence for the orthodox Marxist interpretation.

Industrialization changes things in some important ways. In the last quarter of the century, the first stirrings of industrialization in the South improved the economic position of poor whites, enabling them to institute the Jim Crow system as a means to minimize economic competition from Blacks. Thus, Wilson says, a split-labor market theory becomes more readily applicable.

These changes don't affect the role of the polity in any essential way. In either period, the polity operated basically as reinforcement for patterns of racial dynamics generated by economic factors. It is in the more industrialized North that Wilson finds clearer evidence for his claims about the autonomy of the polity. After something of a honeymoon period just prior to the turn of the century, race relations there came to be dominated by economic competition, with the antagonisms reinforced by competition in the social order, particularly by competition over housing. (Note that competition for housing has become "social," i.e., non-economic.) Here, however, the political system remained neutral, neither reinforcing racial stratification nor mediating racial conflict. To assume a more active role, politicians would have had to put themselves against either the interests of industrial owners or those of white workers.

Throughout this discussion, the principles of general theory are restated in the form of calls for

greater theoretical eclecticism, for greater historical
specificity in the application of theory and warnings
against static, one-variable analysis. This is probably
the most significant contribution of the work, but the
execution is less than satisfying. The discussion of the
antebellum period treats the political hegemony of the
aristocracy as a given, as if how a small, land-holding
class manages to politically neutralize a much larger,
generally enfranchised group should be self-evident.
The discussion of post-war industrialization in the
South is similarly uninformative. Despite some brief il-
lustrative comments drawing primarily on the work of
C. Vann Woodward, there is really little here that one
could call a discussion of the issue. At best, we are left
with a vague sense of the extent and pace of the process, of the evidence suggesting that industrial job competition had consequences different from those
associated with the agricultural sector, and of the
means by which the presumably improved economic
status of white workers led to increased· political
resources. It is certainly not immediately clear that the
skill requirements of some of the industries mentioned
in passing -- turpentine, textiles, tobacco factories --are
such as to create a class of skilled workers indispensable
to the production process. Wilson does refer to the
greater ease of organization associated with industrialization, but that point also is not discussed in
any detail, so that this discussion is no more satisfying
than the treatment given to the same problem by Marx
in the *Manifesto*. The pervasive lack of depth in this
segment of Wilson's argument stands in sharp contrast
to the detail and precision of his discussion of the
migration from the South, a discussion which is only
background, since it raises no issues either empirically
or theoretically problematic.

    This is all the more perplexing since it is not ob-
vious that Wilson needs to raise the issue of industrialization at all. The line of reasoning that he

seems to want to pursue does require that poorer whites have a sense of racial threat, but the situation in the post-war South certainly offers several possible bases for that other than industrialization, possibilities that Wilson treats parenthetically or ignores.

In the end, what have we learned about the utility of a Marxist as opposed to a split-labor theory of racial inequality? Less than one might think. In a summary statement on page 60, he repeats his feelings that the Marxist explanation "is restricted" to the antebellum period and the years immediately following the war while the split-labor theory "...can only be used to explain racial stratification in the late antebellum North and the origins of Jim Crow segregation in the post-bellum South." On the same page, also in reference to the Jim Crow system he says:

The racial caste system ... was solidified both by the ruling class's support of disfranchisement and by the working class's drive (with tacit approval of the ruling class) toward racial exclusiveness in occupation, education, and political power.

If one maintains that the post-war ruling class supported disfranchisement, worked to divide the working class along racial lines (p. 54), and at least tacitly approved of the drive toward racial exclusion, one has already conceded the spirit, if not the letter, of the economic elite thesis. What seems called for is some compromise between that thesis and the split-labor theory.

Turning back to the analysis of twentieth-century race relations, we have already alluded to the fact that Wilson sees the central dynamic there as the way in which class conflict between white workers and white management produced racial conflict between white and Black workers while hamstringing the polity. As Blacks were increasingly absorbed into the unions, particularily in the wake of New Deal legislation, the basis for racial antagonism was significantly reduced. Nevertheless, this did not translate into greater Black access to the ethnically-controlled political machines, depriving Blacks of the "politicization of ethnicity" experienced by other groups, i.e., of the use of ethnic patterns and identity as the foundation for interest group politics (p. 81). In consequence, the pre-war political style of urban Blacks was dominated to an unusual extent by a middle-class elite since the absence of integration with the machines also meant an absence of pressures that would have forced vertical integration of the elite with the Black masses.

Thus, Wilson's argument about the racial neutrality of the polity prior to WW II is intended to apply only to the national political structure. To the extent that the courts sanctioned restrictive convenants, separate-but-equal policies and the like throughout much of this period, the argument should be narrowed further still. More importantly, Wilson's summary statements concerning the machines again seem difficult to reconcile with his description. He says both that "...this racial oppression had no direct connection with or influence on race relations in the private industrial sector"(p. 149) and that it meant Blacks were excluded from patronage jobs and government contracts and services (p. 85). Unless we adopt a stringent definition of "direct connection" -- and it is not certain that we ought, given Wilson's purposes --the two statements are at least potentially at variance. Near-exclusion from one of the avenues of mobility that had been significant for other groups implies that Blacks were relatively more dependent on the private industrial sector, and that certainly should have had some implications for the quality of race relations within that sector, however indirect.

Here we have a lesser example of one of the greater problems in Wilson's analysis, the problem of interconnections. How shall we conceptually separate the economic category from others? How direct need a connection between categories be before we define it as relevant? Wilson's failure to adequately handle these questions bedevils his entire analysis, including his attempt to demonstrate the autonomy of the political system after World War II.

The attempt is straightforward enough. The weakening of political machines and the increasing size of the Black urban population in the North enabled Blacks to exert increasing pressure on government, reflected in more progressive policies from Washington in the 1940's. Ultimately, under the impetus of the Civil Rights Movement, the Federal Government embarked on policies designed to promote racial equality, much in contrast to its racial neutrality prior to the war and its tendency to support racial inequality prior to the turn of the century.

Wilson can fairly be accused of sketchy characterization here. A case can be made that during the same period, the Federal Government pursued housing, urban development and transportation policies that worked disproportionately to the disadvantage of Blacks. What Washington giveth with the one hand, it taketh away quietly with the other. Still, relative to its role in earlier eras, Wilson's characterization is within reason. The explanation is more questionable.

First we have to raise some empirical questions about the significance imputed to Black voting power. Wilson has no discussion of the evidence suggesting that the increasingly progressive policies coming out of Washington after 1940 were responses to changes in voting power. Alternative explanations are certainly possible. One might argue, for example, that in the wartime atmosphere the threatened possibility of massive demonstrations by Blacks became a more potent tool. Then, too, if Black votes were so important nationally, we might reasonably expect that they were also important locally. Some discussion of that would have added to Wilson's case. Finally, many of the more

important changes in Federal policy were initiated by
the judiciary, often to be greeted with indifference or
hostility by the other branches of government.
Presumably, the judiciary is the branch of government
least likely to be responding to the pressure of votes.

It is the problem of interconnection, though,
which is really interesting. If we grant Wilson's argument, have we learned much about the autonomy of
the political system? If racial policies were becoming
more progressive in response to increasing Black voting
power, that voting power itself was a response to
demographic changes having fundamentally economic
roots. The political repercussions of economic needs
appear to be a poor basis on which to establish the
autonomy of the political system. Of course, we can
write off that argument by saying that the economic influences are entirely indirect. Perhaps that is a
reasonable response, perhaps not. The point is, how do
we decide where to draw the line?

Perhaps the most convincing way to argue for
political autonomy would be to show the political
system successfully moving in one direction despite
economic forces pressuring it in some other direction.
This is precisely what Wilson is *not* arguing. The entire
thrust of his case is that as we move into the post-war
era, the economic basis for racial exclusion is eroded,
eroded for white workers by the changes attendant
upon the integration of unions, eroded for management by the development of labor practices which
made it increasingly difficult to replace troublesome
white labor with cheaper Black labor. These are
Wilson's own arguments, and, given them, it would
seem that the most he wants to say is that weakening
the economic motive for racial inequality is associated,
whether casually or not, with parallel changes in
political policy, all of which seems to call for some summary conceptualization short of "autonomy."

Despite his eclectic intentions, Wilson seems in the

end to be primarily an economic determinist of the narrower sort. This is only partly a matter of arguments advertised as non-economic turning out to be only a step or so removed from economic roots; and only partly a matter of conceptual inadequacies making it difficult to follow some of his distinctions. It is largely a matter of Wilson losing contact with the possibly independent effects of racial belief systems, a point receiving little development after his discussion of the mid-nineteenth century. More broadly, Wilson clearly wants to move the discussion beyond the familiar level of cultural and psychological factors by highlighting structural features of the economy and the polity. We could do with a great deal more of that, but Wilson goes too far. Moving beyond the level of social psychology means adding to it, not leaving it out altogether.

Suppose we grant the proposition that for most of this century, the most important racial tensions have been generated by economic competition. Still, even if one generation learned to hate and to act on that hatred on the shop floor and the picket line, didn't their children learn the same lessons earlier and elsewhere? The dictum of the social psychologists which holds that attitudes toward other groups are learned more through contact with the prevailing attitudes toward that group than from contact, competitive or otherwise, with that group is given much less attention than it deserves in Wilson's analysis. Taking the analysis as a whole, I think it fair to say that Wilson is reducing racism to economic and political rationality channeled by systemic restraints. This seems just about as sophisticated as the old attempts to reduce it to the irrationalities of culture, personality, ignorance; that is, the work is ahistorical, despite the historical format.

Conceptual inadequacies show up with greatest clarity in the special theory, the part of Wilson's argument which sets the declining significance of race in post-WW II America. That discussion is predicated upon his very efficient discussion of certain structural shifts in the American economy and the role of Blacks within it. The war pulled significant numbers of Blacks into manufacturing jobs, but economic changes following the war shifted the emphasis of the national economy from manufacturing to service. The lack of expansion in the goods-producing sector coupled with the high educational and skill requirements of the better-paying jobs in the service sector meant a decrease in the number of desirable job options open to lower-class Blacks. In addition, technological changes made many unskilled workers simply redundant, particularly in an economy where changes in compensation patterns and work rules often make the cost of blue-collar labor more a function of the number of workers employed than of the number of hours worked. Thus, even when demand for labor is high, employers may find it cheaper to pay overtime than to hire more workers. Finally, in the face of protective union legislation and equal employement legislation, it becomes all but impossible for employers to use Blacks as a kind of reserve industrial army. In consequence, the significance of race in labor-management strife is nearly eliminated while lower-class Blacks, more because of their class position than because of their racial background, find themselves locked into the unstable, marginal, and lower-paying jobs.

For Blacks with more education or training, the situation could hardly be more different. Affirmative action programs, especially in areas where labor demand exceeds labor supply, and, more importantly, the growing availability of white-collar positions in the public sector, have created a vastly more favorable job market for educated Blacks. As a result, we may expect a growing gap between them and the Black underclass.

Wilson's discussion of the changing connection between race and the economy may not say very much that is new, but it does offer a provocative interpretation of well-known information. It would be possible, though, to add another dimension to it. In the 1940's Ralph Ellison (1953:299) suggested that the introduction of Northern-style race relations to the American South would make possible the more efficient exploitation of the region's social and economic resources. Since then, of course, what was once the Northern mode of racial interaction has become the national mode and we have witnessed immense growth in the Southern economy. Whether there really is, as Ellison expected, any connection between the two is still very much an open question, open because we have given little thought to the possibility. Hopefully, we can pay more attention to it as we continue to explore the kinds of questions which lead Wilson to conclude that the significance of race is declining.

We should be as clear as we can about what that phrase does *not* mean. Wilson does not mean that the consequences of historical patterns of racism have no significance in the contemporary world; he is quite aware that the dead past lives with us yet, if less than clear about how to fit that into his theoretical scheme. Nor is he saying that contemporary racial discrimination is non-existent or negligible. There is, I think, an almost natural temptation to respond to Wilson by citing recent studies attesting to the continuing vitality of discriminatory patterns, but to do so quite misses his point. Nor is he denying that people continue to use race as a highly salient, often emotional, basis for social identification. He is not even saying that racial tensions are less intense than they once were, only that they have shifted to less important areas.

We have already alluded to the fact that it is not easy to draw a distinction between race-as-social identity and race-as-economic determinant or between the more important and less important categories of racial conflict. A study done a few years ago by Mark

Granovetter (1974) illustrates the problem well. Looking at career patterns among a sample of professional,
technical, and managerial workers from the Boston
area, Granovetter's findings support what most of us
have long suspected: access to jobs, particularly to the
better-paying and more satisfying jobs, depends heavily on personal contacts. So long as race is socially
salient, contact networks will continue to develop
primarily within racial groups, so that social life and
economic life should continue to intersect in some important ways, even in the absence of overt racial
discrimination.

The point of this is not to say "Aha! Your
categories are *not* mutually exclusive. They in-
terpenetrate!". Of course they do, and we expect some
conceptual ambiguity in an ambitious work. It is
because of that ambiguity that we want to take special
care in the development of typological schemes. The
need is all the greater in this case because Wilson is using category labels which are so familiar that one can
easily be seduced into thinking that their conceptual
content needs no elaboration. Careful elaboration
ought, at a minimum, give us some idea about how to
think about the boundaries between categories and
some idea of why the boundaries should be drawn
there. Wilson is not doing this. He is not, for example,
giving us any clear discussion of what he means by
"sociopolitical order," although whatever it may be, we
do know that it includes conflict over residential and
school desegregation and over urban political
resources. This is definition by example. Moreover,
these examples seem to involve conflict over certain
kinds of life-chances, economic life-chances in part. If
that is so, do we really need a distinction between them
and the other life-chances that Wilson puts into his
economic category, whatever he may mean by that?
(My best guess, incidentally, is that for most of the
argument, Wilson is conceiving of the economy as job

acquisition and the machinery related to it, not as, say, control over productive resources or as consumption patterns.)

If Wilson tells us little about what his categories mean, he tells us more about why some of them are more important than others, thereby justifying the contention that the significance of race is declining even while racial antagonism remains high. High though antagonisms may be in the sociopolitical order:

...such antagonism has far less effect on individual and group access to those opportunities and resources that are centrally important for life survival than antagonism in the economic sector. The factors that most severely affected black life-chances in previous years were the racial oppression and antagonism in the economic sector. (p.153)

He then goes on to say that even sociopolitical antagonism is not sociopolitical in its origin since "...the ultimate basis for current racial tension is the deleterious effect of basic structural changes in the modern American economy....", which, is, of course, a materialist interpretation, a curious ending for a work purporting to demonstrate the limited utility of a Marxist paradigm.

We may wonder whether the issue here is really "life survival." We might note as well that Wilson has only the most indirect evidence for the proposition that sociopolitical conflicts have economic roots, but let both points pass. What is more important at the moment is that the argument is simply confusing. If racial antagonisms remain strong, if they continue to express themselves in battles over life-chances, if those battles have ultimately economic roots, what purpose is being seved by this residual category of the sociopolitical order, a category that generally seems to mean little more than "non-economic"? The distinction which at first seems self-evident and harmless begins to appear increasingly arbitrary. If all Wilson wants to say is that certain important outcomes of racial antagonism have become much less predictable than previously, that is all well and good, and it is certainly important, but

making that point requires neither this awkward conceptual trapping nor the conclusion that the
significance of race is declining.

Conceptual awkwardness expresses itself in
another way. Wilson uses terms like racial antagonism,
racial conflict, tension, discrimination, and oppression
as if they were interchangeable. Whether they are so
obviously depends on how one chooses to define them;
but as commonly employed, these terms may tap quite
different dimensions of interracial interaction.
Treating them as synonyms muddles certain fundamental distinctions between the subjective and the
objective, between process and consequence, between
form and content, leaving us with an amnibus conceptualization of racial nastiness.

Let us return to the issue of creeping materialism.
Despite the presumed shift of antagonism from the
economic to the sociopolitical order, Wilson argues (p.
116) that "...the key actors on the racial stage remain
the same," i.e., lower-income whites and lower-income
Blacks. Both groups feel the full impact of the urban
fiscal crisis of increased crime, poorer services and
poorer schools and "Thus, the racial struggle for power
and privilege in the central city is essentially a struggle
between the have-nots."

This seems to call for some response. The interpretation seems rather uncritical for a work concerned
with assessing the utility of a Marxist paradigm, a
paradigm which implies that when we find working
class racial antagonisms we ought consider the
possibilities that they are ultimately expressions of class
relationships. Similarly, Wilson's assertion here that
the working-class have *always been* the key actors seems
at variance with the arguments given in the earlier part
of the book. Such a statement would have appeared
more reasonable, for example, if he had not devoted a
previous section to a fairly extensive discussion of the
extent to which the industrialists of an earlier era or-

chestrated racial antagonism. Here again, the analysis and the description seem to proceed along independent paths.

His discussion of Black-Jewish hostility comes close to suggesting a different interpretation of the class basis of modern racial antagonism. In the aftermath of Bakke, it does not seem unreasonable to suppose that recent changes in racial patterns have created a more realistic basis for racial antagonism among socially privileged whites than had been the case in earlier years. It is my impression, at least, that inceasing numbers of upper-middle whites in many sectors of the economy see Black economic progress as immediately threatening and as fundamentally unfair.

Suppose we accept, for the moment, the contention that racial strife is now essentially a struggle between have-nots. His earlier discussions, of course, tend to portray racial strife as an element in the struggle between haves and have-nots. Such a change would lend itself, among many other possibilities, to the interpretation of racial strife which sees it as either a proxy of or a safety valve for tensions generated by have-have-not class relations. The racial hostilities of white workers prevent their pursuing questions of class as aggressively as they otherwise might. If we are looking for a peg upon which to hang a Marxist interpretation of contemporary racial relations, we could hardly hope to find one more obvious.

As if to redress the balance, Wilson seems to become almost too Marxist in his subsequent discussion of the Civil Rights Movement, imputing to the class factor even greater weight than it deserves. Although he has a different view of the end of the decade, his position is that "Lower-income blacks had little involvement in civil rights politics up to the mid-1960's." Insofar as Wilson wants to say that the leadership of the early non-violent resistance movement was disproportionately middle-class, and that that fact af-

fected the nature of the movements in important ways,
fine. Equating that, however, with "little lower-class involvement" borders on the preposterous. The history
that stretches from Montgomery to Selma is -- possibly
above all else -- a history of the politics of class col-
laboration. Had lower-class Blacks actually had little
involvement in the movement, the movement simply
would not have been. It was they who filled the streets
and the jails, stayed off the busses, and tested the pro-
hibitions against voter registration. All of this was done
at the direction of an elite, assuredly, and relations
across class lines were often uneasy, certainly; but to
leap from that to the propostion that the lower classes
had little involvement is to make a mockery of the
historical record and to lose one of the real keys to
understanding subsequent tensions in American racial
politics. Perhaps Wilson means to say that lower-class
involvement was more episodic than middle-class involvement, which would be more defensible.

    Wilson's contention that the movement ultimately
proved most beneficial to those Blacks already highest
in the scale of social privilege is another matter
altogether. Probably, he should have noted that to the
extent that the movement addressed itself to the
destruction of the institutionalized symbols of racial
stigma, it had important consequences for Blacks ir-
respective of class background. Beyond that, the point
is well taken, especially with reference to its economic
consequences.

    What is striking here is that Wilson can ascribe
the improved economic circumstances of many Blacks
to this history of racial politics in large measure and yet
go on to talk about the declining economic significance
of race. Does that mean that the politics were nonracial or non-significant? Interpreting the consequences of race-conscious activity as proof of the
declining significance of race is ahistoricism of the first
order, on a par with taking the creation of the State of

Israel to herald the declining significance of Judaism. Precisely what seems to have happened is that Blacks have become increasingly skilled at using racial identity to political and economic advantage, at using it as protective cloister, as lever, a process Wilson calls the politicization of ethnicity when it occurs among other groups. It is in this sense that we can argue that race has become increasingly significant, not only as a determinant of Black life-chances, but a as a determinant of white life-chances as well, and many whites seem more aware of this than Professor Wilson.

There is a possible objection here. Isn't much of this simply a problem in semantics? Wilson persists in talking about "the declining significance of race" when in fact he clearly means to say racism, or economic racism or, better still the declining effectiveness of job market racism. Had he used one of the latter, less grand, phrases, would not much of the confusion have been prevented and would not the reactions to the work have been less extreme?

No. This line of reasoning will not answer at all. One has to suspect that the problem cuts much more deeply than less felicitous phrasing. There is, I maintain, a long tradition in American scholarship which refuses to see in the phenomenon of race much more than unmitigated misery and unchanging impotence. It is nearly always the case with Wilson that in summary analytical statements what is central about race for him is the way in which whites use it self-consciously as a tool of suppression. How Blacks use race becomes an issue in some of his descriptive statements, but only there. No matter what language one chooses, it seems dangerous for a work whose main business is untangling the webs that tie race to life-chances to proceed from so one-sided a vision of racial processes. Some of the better recent works on race are founded upon a much more complex view of the problem. With all due respect for the empirical quality of Gutman's analysis

of the slave family (1976), what makes the work in-
structive is primarily its angle of vision, the fact that
Gutman complements the familiar query "What did
slaves do with what was done to them?". The same
sense of race as a two-way process undergirds Levine's
(1977) work on Black folk culture or, to reach back
some, Ellison's criticisms of the social science of his day
(1953). At this juncture, any work remaining insensitive to these varied warnings takes us a long way
backwards, and it is largely by remaining insensitive
that Wilson is able to come out at "the declining
significance of race."

But even if the interpretation of the process is less
than satisfying, is not his description of that process
more or less accurate? That is, is it not reasonable to
assert that the extent to which whites self-consciously,
overtly and successfully use race as grounds for limiting
Black access to the job market is decreasing, even
though we may balk at equating that with the declining significance of race? Well, yes, that is more than
reasonable. Saying that, however, is just not news these
days and is hardly entitled to all the fanfare. Indeed,
the matter has already been approached from other
theoretical perspectives. For some time now, we have
been hearing about institutionalized discrimination.
Defined in various ways, the concept is almost in-
variably associated with the argument that race continues to be a salient element in stratifying processes
despite the fact that it is not used as overtly nor as
deliberately as before. (Knowles and Prewitt: 1969;
Carmichael and Hamilton: 1967; Butler: 1976) I find
the literature developng this theme open to question on
several grounds, but it seems improper for Wilson to
proceed as if it did not exist. Doing so undeservedly,
and, no doubt, unintentionally, gives his work an air of
revelations newly received.

What is new is the argument that class has become
more important than race, but nothing in Wilson

allows us to choose that interpretation over the interpretation suggested by the institutional discrimination school. Wilson is not purporting to actually measure the relative impact of class and race on Black life-chances. More, excepting the discussion of the changes in the structure of the job market, he can be quite vague about the nature of these impersonal class barriers, a point to which we need to give closer attention and a point which takes us back to the adequacy of his conceptualization.

Mr. Wilson is quite aware that discrimination in residential housing is still common, a point verified by a recent HEW study (Eggers, Reid, *et al:* 1978). That he writes off as a sociopolitical matter. Aside from being questionable categorization on its face, the problem with that, given the recent tendency for new jobs to be located away from residential concentrations of Blacks, is that any restrictions on residential choice may easily translate into restrictions on job access. Moreover, restrictions on residential choice presumably make the perpetuation of inferior inner-city schools more likely, opening a fresh can of worms for Wilson since his arguments about impersonal class barriers attach substantial importance to the low educational credentials among poor Blacks. Despite several references to the poor quality of inner-city schools, he treats the matter as if bad schools in the ghetto simply drop from the heavens, as if we can be sure that nothing racial is operating there. That, to put it as mildly as possible, is premature.

Wilson's position becomes reasonable if we accept model inner-city schools centering on either IQ deficits or cultural deficits, but not if we adopt the models centering on teacher expectations (e.g., Rist: 1977). The latter argument attaches educational outcomes to teacher expectations and there is some reason to believe that these expectations are generated in part by race. Persell's review of the literature (1977: 103-5)

reports seven studies suggesting such a relationship.
One would not want to generalize from the samples used, however; Persell cites two studies finding no such
relationship, and we certainly cannot yet be certain
that teacher expectations really do influence educational outcomes in any important way. With all of this
admitted, it is sufficient for our purposes to note that
we are hardly in a position to conclude that race plays a
negligible role in schooling, which is to say that we are
hardly in a position to characterize schools as impersonal, class barriers.

We can put the possibilities in more general
terms. It is entirely possible, given what we now know,
that the processes sustaining differentials in racial
privilege have become a good deal more fragmented
than they once were. Where previously the transactions
sustaining racial hegemony were largely deliberately
racist interpersonal transactions supported by institutional sanctions, now the pattern tends to be one in
which racial decisions made in one institutional context, and perhaps made without malice, have implications in other contexts, including the economic one,
which serve to sustain racial inequality. Insofar as the
process is fragmented across institutional boundaries,
and thus stripped of some of its interpersonal and emotional character, we may speak of the rationalization of
inequality in much the same sense that we speak of the
rationalization of work. Wilson's data are too gross to
offer a test of such a model, but nothing in his argument suggests that a model of this sort could not be applied to the changes which concern him, and a model
centering on fragmentation is quite consistent with
some of the assumptions we normally make about the
distinctive quality of social relationships under conditions of modernity. Additionally, such a model leaves
open the fascinating possibility that race not only continues to operate as a sorting-out mechanism, but that
it does so, given its fragmented and non-emotional

quality, in a fashion relatively unlikely to generate grounds for focused resentment. Thus, the response to the politicization of race may consist of concessions which are likely to be depoliticizing in their consequences.

Drawing on the same tradition, we would also expect a shift in the relative importance of ascribed and achieved status criteria. This does not mean that ascription suddenly becomes irrelevant in the world, but it does mean that we would no longer expect to find the extremely high correlations between ascriptive characteristics and life-chances that we often find in the prerationalized world. For the present problem, this would mean that class should become more important in some respects, while race continues to be salient to different degrees in different interactional contexts. Above all, such a model, rather than making arbitrary distinctions among social categories and trying to assess their relative importance, implies that it is the interplay among the categories, the connections in a fragmented process, which are most important.

On balance, what shall we make of this work? We have here, in its general theory, a work which wants to look at the intersection of race and life-chance as a changing, evolving phenomenon. We have a work which refuses to leave the analysis at the attitudinal level, which warns us against overcommitment to any single paradigm. Few academics since Franklin Frazier have reminded us so forcefully that the American racial experience has been a highly variegated one, and is rapidly becoming more so.

We also have a work seriously flawed in execution, sketchy in its historical treatment, somewhat awkward and narrow in its conceptualization, just plain careless in its language, seemingly self-contradictory in part, holding to a rather simplistic view of racial interaction which is neither thoughtful nor thought-provoking. It is, despite the disavowals, a work which holds so rigidly

to a single theoretical viewpoint throughout most of the
argument as to jettison whatever relevant lessons are to
be gleaned from several decades of social psychological
work. The insensitivity to alternate explanations and to
the limitations of the data would by themselves suggest
an unbecoming lack of intellectual humility, but attempting to address these questions in one hundred
and fifty-three pages is nothing short of hubris. In
short, what we have here is neither uninteresting nor
unpromising taken as a first draft, but it constitutes
rather an indifferent book.

Any summary judgment must remain arguable.
Grant me this one momentarily for the sake of allowing
us to speculate very briefly on the meaning of the reactions to the book, since the judgment, if roughly accurate, would imply that there is nothing in the content of the work to justify either the uncritical praise
coming from some audiences, or the unrelieved
criticism coming from others. Even if it did not seem
slightly dishonest to proceed as if that question did not
hover over all of this, we might suppose that any theory
which convincingly explicates the changing nexus between race and economics will necessarily shed some
light on these reactions as well. The one as much as the
other seems to have something to do with the increasing politicization of race. We have to presume, that is,
that the ractions reflect something more than just the
usual differences in professional judgment and even
something more than that selective perception which
leaves the privileged, or those somehow identified with
them, ready to perceive the arrival of the millenium in
every minor change while those whose worldviews are
shaped elsewhere tend to see partial change as mere
palliative, as a potential excuse for no further change.

We might expect that the tradition of equating
race with degradation and impotence would eventually
generate its own counterdynamic, but the more important factors seem to have come from outside the

academy. The politicization of race meant that it was invested with increasingly moral and antagonist overtones and more and more associated with the idea that change is a matter of privilege giving up something tangible, not a matter of privilege softening its heart and issuing soothing pronouncements of goodwill. Thinking about race in such an atmosphere becomes threatening and unsettling, perhaps more so for academics than for most others. Wilson offers a way out. Why, it's not race after all; it's just plain, old class. The sigh of relief at the thought that maybe now they will stop waving the bloody shirt is all but audible. Similarly, the vision of Wilson's harshest critics may be affected by their fear of losing an ideological weapon. Should that be the case, chances are that the weapon they fear to lose is one which has already lost its potency, more now a comforting anachronism than anything else.

Be that as it may, though, the depth of the disparity of judgment about this work suggests that the dialogue of the deaf will be with us a while longer.

REFERENCES

Bonacich, Edna. "A theory of Ethnic Antagonism: The Split-Labor Market." *American Sociological Review,* October, 1972.

Bonacich, Edna. "Advanced Capitalism and Black-White Race Relations in the U.S.". *American Sociological Review,* February, 1976.

Butler, John. "Inequality in the Military". *American Sociological Review,* October 1976.

Carmichael, Stokely and Charles Hamilton. *Black Power.* Vintage: New York, 1967

Elkins, Stanley. *Slavery.* University of Chicago Press: Chicago, 1959.

Ellison, Ralph. *Shadow and Act.* Collier: New York, 1953.

Eggers, F., C. Reid, J. Simonson and R. Wienk. "Background Information and Initial Findings of the Housing Market Practices Survey." U.S. Department of Health, Education, and Welfare: Washington, D.C., 1978.

Granovetter, Mark. *Getting A Job.* Harvard Press: Cambridge, 1974.

Gutman, Herbert. *The Black Family In Slavery and Freedom: 1750-1925.* Pantheon: New York, 1976.

Knowles, L. and K. Prewitt. *Institutional Racism In America.* Prentice-Hall: Englewood Cliffs, New Jersey, 1969.

Levine, Lawrence. *Black Culture and Black Consciousness.* Oxford: New York, 1977.

Persell, Caroline. *Education and Inequality.* Free Press: New York, 1977.

Rist, Ray. "On Understanding the Processes of Schooling: The Contributions of Labeling Theory." In J. Karabel and A. H. Halsey (eds.), *Power and Ideology In Education.* Oxford: New York, 1977.

12

THE CONTINUING SIGNIFICANCE OF A RACIALLY DUAL SOCIETY

By

*Bernard M. Kramer, Department of Psychology,
University of Massachusetts at Boston*

An old debate has recently reemerged concerning the significance of race in American life. Associated with the name of William Wilson, it occurs in the context of a nation paradoxically polarized while yearning for an end to divisiveness. Many will remember the poster of 1968 appealing to the new president: "Bring us together." But the very election of that president signalled the advent of an anti-Black sentiment clearly different from the supportive mood that aided the forward surge of the civil rights movement in the preceding decade. Advances in the legal, political and economic spheres have led some to believe that the struggle has been won and that the back of American racism has been broken. What remains, in this view, is only to solve the problem of poverty and class distinctions. Not race but class is the issue.

I and others, however, hold that Blacks in the United States remain a despised people. Progress, we concede, has clearly occurred and, indeed, the size of the Black middle class has increased. But Black existence is still shaped by massive discrimination, segregation and poverty. Accordingly, the United States is correctly characterized as a dual society on racial lines. Only the details of this dual society have changed, not its basic nature.

The issue is undoubtedly complex and definitive answers are hard to come by. It is nonetheless a matter of gravely serious dimensions that requires reasoned attention informed by an awareness that the nation's foremost domestic problem is at stake.

I think of the words engraved in a monument at Boston's Park Square memorializing Lincoln's Emancipation Proclamation: "A race set free and the country at peace. Lincoln rests from his labors." It teaches us, ironically, that the socio-economic status of descendants of slaves in the United States today is the outcome of the nation's failure to establish a permanent basis for full equality after the abolition of slavery. Numerous compromises along with legal and semi-formal restrictions established instead a malignant moral equivalent of slavery. In the South it was the post-Plessy Jim Crow laws governing almost every conceivable piece of human behavior. In the North it was, and is, the widespread practice of residential segregation on racial grounds. Additionally there was the failure to incorporate former slaves and their descendants in land distribution, such as that exemplified by the Homestead Act. Moreover, Blacks were virtually excluded from the vast industrialization that occurred in the late nineteenth century.

These are all well-known facts that bear repetition here only because they help us recognize that historic failures lie behind what is today incontrovertible, i.e., the United States is a dual society made up of Whites at the top and Blacks at the bottom. Nuances and subtleties, to be sure, complicate the picture. The outlines of the picture, however, are bold and unarguable. In education, in income, in occupation, in housing, in every sphere imaginable, Whites are ahead and Blacks are behind; Whites are superordinate and Blacks are subordinate. Until this fundamental scene is altered, our society must be characterized as a racially dual society. In this sense, then, the continuing significance of race and racism must be seen as central to a properly illuminated analysis of our society. Likewise, actions aimed at achieving our most fondly hoped-for goals must take into account the deeply racial dimensions of our society.

A brief glance at the long history of anti-Semitism may help us gain some perspective. The remarkable thing about anti-semitism is not so much its blood-curdling longevity and intensity as is the variety of its expression and the cyclicity of its occurrence. Jews have been expelled, massacred, confined, ghettoized, stigmatized, restricted, terrorized, calumnified and, finally, in our day, incinerated. This fantastic range of negative actions occurred over the centuries, however, with a characteristic ebb and flow. A series of expulsions from France in the 14th century, for example, was followed by an attendant series of returns. Highly favored status in Spain and Poland preceded exceptionally intense hatred. We may say with confidence that in the history of anti-Semitism there has been a waxing and waning that should give us pause for concern in our present assessment of the significance of race in American life. For we learn that appearances may very well be deceiving. What appears in our statistical tables as progress may turn out to be a prologue to trouble. Favored treatment to correct past injustice may be followed by a return to that very past. Long standing animosities die hard. They should not be ignored despite apparent but impermanent advances.

Advances associated with 1960's occurred during a period in which the term, "economy of abundance" was in the wind. The War on Poverty, the Great Society, the Civil Rights Movement were all highly thinkable and supportable because there was an air of optimism suffusing the social and economic thought of the time. There was, it was thought, more than enough to go around. Not just enough, but more than enough. This meant that large segments of the American people believed that hitherto mistreated minority groups were not only entitled to a better shake, but that it could all be easily afforded. It was not, however, a clearly articulated, nor consciously stated, belief. Yet, prosperity was widespread enough so that the argument of justice and fairness was not seriously challenged by the argument of economics and feasibility.

In the 1970's, on the other hand, there is an altogether different sense of what is possible and what is not. No longer do people think there is more than enough. On the contrary, the question is raised as to whether there is enough at all. One hears talk now of "economy of scarcity" and "no growth economy". The press for environmental protection and the conservation of nature has been accompanied by an attitude of limitation and constraint together with a sense of competition for scarce resources. For minorities of color this changed circumstance is a matter of grave concern.

The task of gaining enduring system-wide advances is increasingly difficult as the political-economic context becomes tighter and tighter. It is no accident that the Bakke and Weber cases have come to pass during this restrictive period and that concerned members and supporters of the minority communities view developments in these and related cases with greatest apprehension. One has to wonder whether the current attack on affirmative action for equal opportunity is not analogous with the ultimately successful efforts to dismantle the post-Civil War Reconstruction. If this is true, then it is likely that our society will steadily evolve toward greater fixity in its racially dual qualities. While public attitudes toward integration have steadily become more favorable, actual practices have become more conducive to segregation particularly in the sphere of residential housing. In short, we are living in a racially dual society with prospects for improvement highly problematic.

Just as the United States is the dominant force in the world at large, so are White Euro-Americans the dominant force in the United States. The progress that has been made by some Blacks should not obscure the basic dimensions of the picture we see today: the vast majority of Blacks and Third World people remain as an alien and separate presence in American life, seething with discontent and with no visible avenue open for positive, constructive action. Suffering continues and the basic conditions exist for a divided, violent and repressive society. The self-interest of masses of Blacks and Whites calls for the creation of a unitary society based on the universal application of the principles of racial justice and equality. The creation of such a society is seriously impeded by the false assertion that it already exists.

SUMMARY
AND
CONCLUSION

13

THE INCLINING SIGNIFICANCE OF RACE*

By

Charles V. Willie

Commentary prepared for *Society* magazine, July/August, 1978, in response to an excerpt from *The Declining Significance of Race* by William J. Wilson that was published in the January/February issue.

It is all a matter of perspective. From the perspective of the dominant people of power, inequality exists because of the personal inadequacies of those who are less fortunate. Varying degrees of fortune is the essence of the social stratification system in this nation. In America, it is the affluent rather than the poor who use social class theory to explain poverty. Moreover, they assert that poverty is not a function of institutional ar rangements but a matter of individual capacities. From the perspective of the dominant people of power, the social stratification system in the United States is open and any who has the capacity can rise within it. This orientation toward individual mobility tends to mask the presence of opportunities that are institutionally based such as attending the "right" school, seeking employment with the "right" company or firm,

and being of the "right" race. Also this orientation
toward individual mobility tends to deny the presence
of opposition and oppression that are connected with
institutions. According to the perspective of the dominant people of power, opportunity and especially
educational and economic opportunity is a function of
merit.

William Julius Wilson has used the perspective of
the dominant people of power in his article on "The
Declining Significance of Race" that appeared in the
January/February edition of Society. An individual,
including a scholar in the social sciences, is free to use
any perspective that he or she wishes to use. The tradition of friendly criticism in this field, however, supports the effort which I shall undertake in this commentary. My purpose is to make explicit that which is
implicit so that others may assess the conclusions of
Professor Wilson on the basis of the premises and the
perspective of his analysis.

At the end of his article which asserts that "Class
has become more important than race in determining
black life chances in the modern indistrial period,"
Professor Wilson tries to disassociate himself from the
individualism of the dominant people of power by call-
ing for "public policy programs to attack inequality on
a broad class front--policy programs, in other words,
that go beyond the limits of ethnic and racial
discrimination by directly confronting the pervasive
and destructive features of class subordination." The
action which Professor Wilson calls for ignores the interconnection between race and social class as a complex of interrelated characteristics and further does not
take cognizance of the fact that there may be a serial
pattern to the solution to social problems.

COMPLEX OF CHARACTERISTICS

An historic example is given. One reason that

other scholars did not discover the laws of population genetics before Mendel is that "they treated as units the complexes of characteristics of individuals, races and species and attempted to find rules governing inheritance of such complexes," according to Theodosius Dobzhansky. "Mendel was the first to understand that...the inheritance of separate traits [and] not [the inheritance of] complexes of traits...had to be studied." With reference to the community and processes of social change, Susan Greenblatt and I have pointed out in an article entitled, "A New Approach to Comparative Community Analysis" that maybe it is the other way around. "It is possible that we may successfully understand school desegregation [or poverty and race relations] by using a method that analyzes complexes of characteristics." Professor Wilson attempts to analyze the relationships between the races in the United States in terms of individual traits rather than as a complex of characteristics. The traits in which he is most interested have to do with the economy. Professor Wilson acknowledges that "in the modern industrial period race relations have been shaped as much by important economic changes as by important political changes," but then he denies the significance of this complex by stating the following: "...ingenious schemes of racial exploitation, discrimination, and segregation,...however significant they were in the creation of poverty-stricken ghettos and a vast underclass of black proletarians...do not provide a meaningful explanation of the life chances of black Americans today." He goes on to say that the significance of the association between "race and economic class only" has grown as the nation has entered the modern industrial period.

While making this assertion, Professor Wilson acknowledges that "the presence of blacks is still firmly resisted in various institutions and social arrangements, for example, residential areas and private social

clubs." By attempting to isolate the economic sphere
from the other institutions and social arrangements of
society, Professor Wilson has committed the error of
particularism, an error committed by many social
scientists who attempt to model analysis of the social
system after the organic system, who attempt to
analyze traits rather than the complex of
characteristics. Evidence from other studies have
demonstrated an association between economic opportunity, educational opportunity, and residential location. This is what the current movement for school
desegregation and the resistance to busing are all
about. Thus, resistance to the presence of blacks in
residential areas, for example, cannot be dismissed as
irrelevant to social mobility in the economic sphere.

My own study of the "Relative Contribution of
Family Status and Economic Status to Juvenile Delinquency" that was published in *Social Problems* in 1967
illuminates the serial approach to the solution of social
problems. In summary, I found "In Washington,
D.C., 80 percent of the white population lives in
economically affluent areas while 67 percent of the
nonwhite population lives in neighborhoods of poverty
or marginal economic condition. Since poverty was no
longer an overwhelming problem for most white people, family instability was a major remaining and
outstanding problem contributing to the incidence of
juvenile delinquency. Although the percent of non-
white children growing up in one-parent families was
greater than the percent of white children who had this
kind of experience, the impoverished economic circumstances of nonwhites was overwhelming. In the
light of the data...[I] hypothesized that nonwhites may
be able to deal with the family instability factor which
is associated with juvenile delinquency only after
notable improvements have been experienced in their
economic circumstances. The hypothesis is advanced
on the basis of the findings...pertaining to the white

population which is largely beyond the pale of poverty."

SERIAL PATTERN

Out of this analysis I extracted the principle that the solutions of some social problems occur in a serial pattern, that the solution to one problem makes possible the solution of another. There is an ordering of social events into a sequential pattern. Most whites have passed beyond the stage of economic insecurity. Thus strengthening their families is the most significant way to further reduce delinquency in the white population. But efforts to strengthen family ties and increase family stability among blacks probably will not be very successful until opportunities for economic upgrading are provided. This assertation was based on the findings that 40 percent of the variance in the family instability factor could be attributed to socioeconomic status at that time in Washington.

Thus, I concluded that "this society may have the possibility of helping a population achieve greater family stability...only after it has assisted a population to achieve greater economic security." *Not only are most social problems a complex of characteristics such as that of juvenile delinquency, socioeconomic status, and race, but also their solution must be approached in a sequential way. Clearly the public policy of strengthening the black family as a way of overcoming

---

*I did not state explicitly the connection between economic insecurity and racial discrimination in this commentary. I assumed that it was self-evident. However, Wilson's response to this commentary indicates that what was implicit should have been made explicit. Thus as a footnote, added in this reprinted commentary, I include a statement from my book on *Church Action in the World* (1969, pp. 6-7) that comments upon these data about delinquency that were gathered in Washington: "We are not going to do anything about delinquency in our society unless we do something about poverty; and we are not going to do very much about poverty unless we do something about racial...discrimination."

various forms of pathology that was advocated by
Daniel Patrick Moynihan, first, was a projection most
appropriate for whites upon blacks, and second, was a
violation of the sequential approach to social problem-
solving. Neither social scientists nor public
policymakers are free to pick and choose points of intervention that they prefer, if they wish to be effective.
Professor Wilson, for example, may wish to focus on
the economic sphere and social class as a way of dealing
with inequality. But racial discrimination and oppression in "various institutions and social arrangements"
may require intervention in these areas first.

Professor Wilson suggests that changes in many
spheres, other than economic, already have occurred
in previous stages which he has designated as stage one,
the *plantation economy* and *racial-caste oppression;*
stage two, *industrial expansion, class conflict* and
racial oppression and stage three, during the 1960s and
1970s, *progressive transition from race inequalities to
class inequality.* My contention is that the transition is
far from complete for upper-class, middle-class,
working-class, and under-class blacks, and that barriers to economic opportunity still are largely a function of discrimination based on race and sex.

The remainder of this discussion will demonstrate
this fact with data and point out errors in the analysis
of William Julius Wilson that may be a function of the
perspective used that probably caused him to miss
some essential information.

INCOME

First, let us look at income. As recent as 1975, the
median income for white families was $14,268 com-
pared with a median of $9,321 for blacks and other
minority races. This means that blacks and other racial
minorities received only two-thirds as much income as
did whites. At both ends of the income scale, the ratio

of black to white income was about the same. Under $5,000 a year there was only 10.2 percent of the white families and individuals compared with 26.3 percent of the population of black families and individuals. Earning $25,000 a year and over in 1975, was 15.1 percent of the white population compared with 6.4 percent of the black population. The proportion of blacks who were very poor was two and one-half times greater than the proportion of whites who were very poor; and the proportion of whites who were most affluent was two and one-third times greater than the proportion of blacks with high incomes. There is not much of a difference in these income ratios by race for the poor and the affluent. In general, the proportion of high-income blacks is far less than what it would be if there was no racial discrimination. The 1977 report, *All Our Children,* by the Carnegie Council on Children of which Kenneth Keniston was senior author states that "90 percent of the income gap between blacks and whites is the result...of lower pay for blacks with comparable levels of education and experience." Despite this and other findings such as those presented by economist Herman Miller in his book *Rich Man, Poor Man,* Professor Wilson states that "many talented and educated blacks are now entering positions of prestige and influence at a rate comparable to or, in some situations, exceeding that of whites with equal qualifications."

In 1974, 15 percent of the white male population was of the professional or technical workers category compared with 9 percent of the male population of blacks and other minority races. This appeared to be a notable change relative to whites but it represented only an increase of 3 percentage points over the 6 percent of black and other minority males who were professionals 10 years earlier. Moreover, only 5 percent of the black and other racial minority males were managers and administrators in 1974 compared with 15 percent of all white employed males. In summary, 42 percent of the white male population was white collar in 1974 compared with 24 percent of the racial minority males in this nation. These data indicate that blacks have a long way to go before they catch up with whites in high-level occupations.

Moreover, a study by the Survey Research Center of the University of Michigan that was published in the *New York Times* February 26, 1978, reported that 61 percent of all blacks in a nationwide poll believed that whites either don't care whether or not blacks "get a break" or were actively trying to keep blacks down. It would appear that neither the sentiment of blacks nor the facts of the situation are in accord with the analysis of Professor Wilson and his claim that "class has become more important than race in determining black life chances."

The University of Michigan study also found that one out of every two white persons believed that "few blacks...miss out on jobs and promotions because of racial discrimination." This response is similar to the conclusion of Professor Wilson and is the reason why I stated earlier that his analysis was from the perspective of the dominant people of power.

EDUCATION

Second, let us look at what is happening to poor blacks to determine whether their circumstances are more a function of social class than of race. This analysis, I believe, reveals a fundamental error in the analysis of Professor Wilson--an error no less serious than that committed by Daniel Patrick Moynihan and Christopher Jencks who made observations on whites and projected these upon blacks. Howard Taylor, a sociologist and expert methodologist, has stated that Jencks took "considerable liberties in discussing the effects of integration, segregation, race, etc., upon occupational and income inequality. He clearly infers that education is not related to success for black people; that if blacks want more money, then more education will not get it. But this inference is based upon path analysis done only on native white non-farm males who took the armed forces IQ test! Who can say that causal models and estimates based on native white non-farm males are applicable to blacks? Not one single path analysis in the entire report is performed on even one black sample." Howard Taylor made these observations in an article entitled "Playing the Dozens with Path Analysis" that was published the *Sociology of Education* in 1973.

It is obvious that Professor Wilson has analyzed the job situation for affluent blacks. The census data that I reported earlier indicated that blacks were catching up with whites, relatively, so far as employment in the professions is concerned. While the proportion of white male professionals a decade ago was twice as great as the proportion of black and other minority male professionals, the proportion as late as 1974 was only two-thirds greater. On the basis of data like these, Professor Wilson states that "talented and educated blacks are experiencing unprecedented job opportunities in the growing government and corporate sectors." After analyzing the "job situation for the more privileged blacks," Professor Wilson projects these findings upon the poor and says "it would be difficult to argue that the plight of the black underclass is solely the consequence of racial oppression, that is, the explicit and overt efforts of whites to keep blacks subjugated...."

While the facts cited earlier cast doubt upon the conclusion that talented blacks are experiencing "unprecedented job opportunities," even if one accepts the modest improvement for "talented blacks" as fact, it is inappropriate to project middle class experience upon the underclass of blacks. This is precisely what Professor Wilson has done.

His assertion that "the black experience has moved historically from economic racial oppression experienced by virtually all blacks to economic subordination for the black under-class" cancels out racial
discrimination as a key cause of poverty among blacks.
If one assumes that there are not extraordinary
biological differences between blacks and whites in the
United States, then it is difficult to explain why the
proportion of poor blacks with an annual income
under $5,000 is two and one-half times greater than
the proportion of poor whites. Among poor white
youth and young adults the unemployment rate is
higher for high school dropouts than for persons who
graduated from higher schools but did not receive
more education.   Among blacks, however, the
unemployment rate is high and is the same for high
school dropouts and for those who graduated from
high school but did not receive more education. Staying in high school seems not to make a difference for
blacks so far as the risk of unemployment is concerned.

Among whites with only an elementary school
education or less, 50 percent are likely to have jobs as
service workers or laborers at the bottom of the occupational heap; but 80 percent of black workers with this
limited education are likely to find work only in these
kinds of jobs. This was what Herman Miller found in
his analysis of 1960 census data. These facts indicate
that education alone cannot explain the disproportionate number of blacks in low-paying jobs. If the
absence of education is the basis for limited upward
mobility in the stratification system, why do whites
with little education get better jobs than blacks?

Using 1968 data, Miller analyzed the difference in
median income for whites and blacks and other non-
white minorities. He found that the difference for the
races ranged from $880 for those who had completed
grade school only to $2,469 for those who had attended

or graduated from college. Median income by schooling not only differed by race but tended to widen between the racial groups with increase in education. On the bases of these findings, Miller said that "there is some justification for the feeling by Puerto Ricans, Negroes, and other minority groups that education does not do as much for them financially as it does for others." These findings Miller reported in the 1971 edition of his book, *Rich Man, Poor Man,* and they indicated that racial discrimination is a contributing factor to the occupational opportunities and income received by poor as well as affluent blacks.

RESIDENTIAL SEGREGATION

With reference to residential segregation which Professor Wilson wants to ignore as irrelevant, he has received modest support from the findings of Albert Simkus that were reported in the February 1978 edition of the *American Sociological Review* in an article entitled "Residential Segregation by Occupation and Race in Ten Urbanized Areas, 1950-1970." Simkus said that "historically, blacks with high incomes have been as highly or more highly segregated from whites with similar incomes than have low-income blacks." This fact became "slightly less true...by 1970." However, Simkus attributes the slight change to political rather than economic factors. Particularly singled out for credit is civil rights and housing legislation of the 1960s.

Simkus points out that the decrease in residential segregation of affluent blacks is beginning to catch up with the integrated residential areas that characterized lower-income blacks and whites in the past. Specifically, he said that "apart from the comparisons involving nonwhite professionals, nonwhites and whites in the lowest occupational categories were still slightly less segregated than those in the higher categories."

Finally, I call attention to the fact that Professor Wilson's data are at variance with the clinical observations of other blacks. The unprecedented job opportunities simply have not been experienced by some talented and educated blacks. During the summer of 1977, *The New York Times* published an interview with Sanford Allen, a black violinist with the New York Philharmonic Orchestra. Allen announced his intention to resign from his position. He said that he was "simply tired of being a symbol." At that time, Allen was the only black who had been a member of the 133-year-old musical organization. He charged the more prestigious symphony orchestras of this nation, such as the Boston Symphony, the Chicago Symphony, and two or three others, with running a closed shop that excluded blacks. Allen joined the New York Philharmonic in 1962. During a decade and a half, no other blacks had been hired. A story like this one, of course, is clinical evidence and does not carry the same weight as research evidence systematically gathered. But such clinical evidence has been accumulating recently and deserves to be looked at carefully.

The response of white professionals to admissions policies by colleges and universities that are designed to reserve spaces for members of previously excluded racial populations in the first-year classes of professional schools is a case in point. The opposition to such practices indicates that talented and educated blacks are not being given access to privilege and power "at a rate comparable to or, in some situations, exceeding that of whites with equivalent qualifications" as Professor Wilson claims. The opposition to special minority admissions programs is led by white professionals, not white hard-hat or blue-collar workers. This is further clinical evidence that race is not irrelevant and has not declined in significance for talented and educated blacks.

COUNTERHYPOTHESIS

Actually, I would like to introduce a counterhypothesis that the significance of race is increasing and that it is increasing especially for middle-class blacks who, because of school desegregation and affirmative action and other integration programs, are coming into direct contact with whites for the first time for extended interaction.

My case studies of black families who have moved into racially integrated neighborhoods and racially integrated work situations, indicate that race for some of these pioneers is a consuming experience. They seldom can get away from it. When special opportunities are created, such as in the admissions programs, the minorities who take advantage of them must constantly prove themselves. When a middle-class black has been accepted as Sanford Allen was in the Philharmonic, the issue then shifts to whether or not one is being used as a symbol. Try as hard as they may, middle-class blacks, especially middle-class blacks in racially integrated situations at this period in American history are almost obsessed with race. Many have experienced this adaption especially in residential and work situations.

Any obsession, including obsession with race, is painful. Freedom is circumscribed and options are delimited not because of physical segregation but because of the psychological situation. So painful is the experience of racial obsession that two extreme reaction are likely to occur. Middle-class blacks may attempt to deal with the obsession by capitulation--that is, by assuming everything is race-related, that all whites are racists, and that all events and circumstances must be evaluated first in terms of their racial implications. The other adaptation is denial, believing that race is irrelevant and insignificant even when there is clear and present evidence that it is not.

This is one of the personal consequences of a racist society for the oppressed as the old separatist system begins to crumble. The people who most severly experience the pain of dislocation due to the changing times are the racial minorities who are talented and educated and integrated, not those who are impoverished and isolated.

READINGS SUGGESTED BY THE AUTHOR

Blau, Peter M. *Inequality and Heterogeneity*. New York: The Free Press, 1977.

Miller, Herman, *Rich Man, Poor Man*. New York: Thomas Crowell, 1964

Simkus, Albert, "Residential Segregation by Occupation and Race in Ten Urbanized Areas, 1950-1970." *American Sociological Reviews* 43 (February 1978): 81-93.

Taylor, Howard F. "Playing the Dozens with Path Analysis." *Sociology of Education* 46 (Fall 1973): 433-50.

Willie, Charles V. *A New Look at Black Families*. Bayside, N.Y.: General Hall, 1976.

14

THE DECLINING
SIGNIFICANCE OF RACE
Revisited But Not Revised*

By

William Julius Wilson

Rejoinder prepared for *Society* magazine, July/August, 1978 in response to the commentary by Charles V. Willie about the excerpt from *The Declining Significance of Race* that was published in the January/February, 1978 issue.

Professor Charles V. Willie says that it is all a matter of perspective. He is wrong, it is also a matter of interpretation. And his interpretation of the excerpts from my book *(Society,* January/February 1978), *The Declining Significance of Race,* erroneously associates what is in fact a macro-sociological argument of inequality with a so-called dominant group perspective of individual mobility.

In my response to Willie's contentions I do not plan to devote much attention to perspectives; the reader can easily make that judgment. Instead, the bulk of this paper will consider the validity of assertions. In the process I hope to demonstrate that, under close scrutiny, not a single one of Willie's "empirical" criticisms can be upheld, and that contrary to his

claims, the data he presents and the counterhypotheses
he proposes neither demonstrate errors in my analysis
nor undermine my arguments on the growing importance of class and the decreasing significance of race in
determining blacks' chances in life.

MACROSOCIOLOGICAL ANALYSIS OF RACE AND CLASS

However, before I directly comment on Willie's
article, I would like, in a few succinct paragraphs, to
put the basic arguments of my book in proper focus.
My book is an attempt to explain race and class in the
American experience. I feel that in order to understand the changing issues of race and, indeed, the relationship between class and race in America, a
framework that would relate changes in intergroup
relations with changes in the American social structure
is required. Individual mobility is not used as the independent variable in explaining race and class experiences, as Willie's analysis would suggest. Rather I
try to show how the economy and state interacted in
different historical periods not only to structure the
relations between blacks and whites and to produce
dissimilar contexts for the manifestation of racial antagonisms, but also to create different situations for
racial group access to rewards and privileges. Using
this framework, I define three stages of American race
relations (the preindustrial, industrial, and modern industrial), stages in which I describe the role of both the
system of production and the state in the development
of race and class relations.

Although my book devotes considerable attention
to the preindustrial and industrial periods of American
race relations, it is my description of the modern industrial period that has generated controversy and has
provoked Willie to respond. I contend that in the
earlier periods, whether one focuses on the way race

relations were structured by the economy or by the state or both, racial oppression (ranging from the exploitation of black labor by the economic elite to the elimination of black competition, especially economic competition, by the white masses) was a characteristic and important aspect of life. However, I also maintain that in the modern industrial period the economy and the state have, in relatively independent ways, shifted the basis of racial antagonisms away from black/white economic contact to social, political, and community issues. The net effect is a growing class division among blacks, a situation, in other words, in which economic class has been elevated to a position of greater importance than race in determining individual black opportunities for living conditions and personal life experiences.

Now, it is difficult to recapture in these few paragraphs the distinctions and arguments presented in *The Declining Significance of Race*, but the preceding synopsis will at least provide the necessary background in considering Willie's interpretation and critique of my thesis.

WILLIE'S ANALYSIS

In fairness to Willie, it should be pointed out that he was responding to the excerpts from my book that appeared in *Society* magazine and therefore did not have the benefit of the full array of data and arguments I use to support my contentions. I will therefore discuss some of these data in the ensuing paragraphs, as well as present some additional facts that were not incorporated in *The Declining Significance of Race*, but which serve to demonstrate the inadequacies of Professor Willie's data.

Willie presents three major arguments: (1) that I "commit the error of particularism" in the sense that I try "to isolate the economic sphere from the other institutions and social arrangements of society"; (2) that barriers to economic opportunites for blacks are still mainly a function of race and that the available data support this contention; and (3) that a counterhypothesis should be proposed, namely that "the significance of race is increasing...especially for middle-class blacks who, because of school desegregation, and affirmative action and other integration programs, are coming into direct contact with whites for the first time for extended interactions."

ERROR OF PARTICULARISM

In response to Willie's charge that I "isolate the economic sphere from the other institutions and social arrangements of society," let me say, first of all, that I would be the last to deny that there is an empirical "association between economic opportunity, educational opportunity, and residential location." Indeed, contrary to Willie's assertion, this complex relationship is demonstrated repeatedly in several chapters of my book. The problem has to do with the direction of the relationship. What I attempt to show is that in the modern industrial period, as economic opportunity for blacks increasingly depends on class affiliation, we see corresponding differences in black educational opportunity and residential location. Thus as the black middle class experiences greater occupational mobility, they, like more privileged whites, abandon public schools and send their children to private schools. Accordingly, public schools in large urban areas are not only suffering from racial isolation: they are also suffering from class isolation. By the same token, higher-income blacks are not trapped in depressed ghettoes and, although they have greater difficulty than middle-class whites in finding housing, their economic resources provide them with more opportunities to find desirable housing and neighborhoods either in the central city or in the suburbs than both lower-income blacks and lower-income whites. On the other hand, the lack of economic opportunity for under-class blacks means that they are forced to attend inferior ghetto schools and remain in economically depressed ghettoes. Ghetto isolation and inferior educational opportunities reinforce their low position in the labor market. This process is a vicious circle and, to repeat, is demonstrated in my book, even though I give more weight to economic opportunities than to noneconomic opportunities.

Furthermore, I agree with Willie's assertion that "efforts to strengthen family ties and increase family stability among blacks probably will not be very successful until opportunities for economic upgrading are provided." Indeed, this is one of the major arguments of chapter six of *The Declining Significance of Race*. For example, I show that in 1974, only 18 percent of the children in black families with incomes of less than $4,000 lived with both parents, while 90 percent of the children in black families of $15,000 or more lived with both parents. I argue, therefore, that "to suggest categorically that the problem of female-headed households is characteristic of black families is to overlook the powerful influence of economic-class background. The increase in female-headed households among poor blacks is a consequence of the fact that the poorly trained and educated black males have increasingly restricted opportunities for higher-paying jobs and thus find it increasingly difficult to satisfy the expectations of being a male breadwinner." If Willie and I do have a real difference of opinion on this matter, it is that he associates the increasing difficulties of the black poor with racial discrimination whereas I maintain (and will further elaborate below) that class restrictions associated with structural shifts in the economy are the more important factors in accounting for poor blacks' limited occupational mobility today.

But Willie is not always consistent in his arguments about the "sequential approach to social-problem solving." On the one hand he argues, as in fact I do, that efforts to strengthen black families will not succeed until economic opportunities are upgraded; yet, on the other hand, he contradicts this position with the statement that "Professor Wilson, for example, may wish to focus on the economic sphere and social class as a way of dealing with inequality. But racial discrimination and oppression in 'various institutions and social arrangements' may require intervention in these areas first." I stand by my contention that the factors that most severely effected black life chances in previous years were racial oppression and antagonism in the economic sector. As race declined in importance in the economic sector, the black class structure became more differentiated and black life chances increasingly became a consequence of class affiliation. This is not to deny the importance of racial antagonism in the social-political order, or even to suggest that residential, social, and educational discrimination do not form a part of a vicious circle that feeds back to the economic sector. But this circular process is far more relevant for poor blacks than for more privileged blacks. In terms of understanding life chances, the economic mobility of privileged blacks has offset the negative consequences of racial discrimination in the social-political order. Indeed, one will only be able to understand the growing class divisions in the black community by recognizing that racial antagonisms in the sociopolitical order have far less effect on black individual or group access to those opportunities and resources that are centrally important for life chances, than have racial antagonisms in the economic sector.

But the bulk of Willie's article concentrates on data he presents to "point out errors" in my analysis. I would now like to examine these data and Willie's interpretation of them.

In an attempt to refute my assertion that class has become more significant than race in determining black life chances, Willie presents data indicating (1) that the median income for black families in 1975 was several thousand dollars less than the median income for white families; (2) that the proportion of black families who were poor (income of less than $5,000 a year) was two and one-half times greater than the proportion of white families who were poor, and the proportion of white families who were affluent (income of $25,000 or more a year) was two and one-third times greater than the proportion of black families who were affluent; (3) that 90 percent of the black-white income gap is the result of lower pay for blacks with comparable experience and education; (4) that in 1968 "median income by schooling not only differed by race but tended to widen between the racial groups with increase in education"; (5) that staying in high school for blacks does not make a difference with respect to the risk of unemployment; and (6) that "42 percent of the white male population was white collar in 1974 compared with 24 percent of racial minority members in the nation."

The problem with these statistics is not that they are inaccurate or even that some are outdated. The problem is that they obscure the very important distinction between the effects of past discrimination and the current effects of race in the economic world. In other words, they allow investigators to either ignore or overlook the importance of a legacy of past discrimination and therefore to interpret the overall black-white gap in income and employment as an indication of present discrimination. The fact that this approach tends to distort the significance of race today is most clearly revealed when we examine the labor market experiences of various subgroups within the black population.

BLACK EDUCATED MALES

There is compelling evidence that young black male college graduates now receive roughly the same salaries as young white men with college degrees. Data from the 1970 Census of Population show that in 1969 black male graduates age 22 to 24 received a slightly higher average income than comparable whites; and more recent findings from the 1973 *Current Population Survey* show that black men with college degrees in the 25 to 29 age category earned close to $1,000 more than their white counterparts. Moreover, the economist Richard B. Freeman found that the starting salaries of male graduates from black colleges in the South in 1968-70 were comparable to the average starting salaries for male college graduates on a national level. These findings, obscured in Willie's gross income comparisons of all college educated blacks and all college educated whites, represent a significant change from the discriminatory pattern of the past whereby black college graduates at all age levels received substantially lower salaries than white college graduates of comparable ages.

But why have young black male college graduates finally reached income parity with young white male college graduates? Because the combination of an increased demand for white-collar salaried employees in the corporate and government sector and the pressures of state antidiscrimination programs, especially affirmative action pressures, have cleared the path for minority college graduates and have allowed them to enter positions of prestige and influence denied to them in the past. We only need to examine the changing racial practices of corporations to see that opportunities for educated blacks have sharply increased. As shown in Freeman's study, the efforts of corporations to

recruit college-trained blacks increased sharply between 1965 and 1970. In fact, the average number of
recruitment visits of representatives of corporations to
predominantly black colleges rose from 4 in 1960 to 50
in 1965 and then climbed to 297 in 1970. And schools
such as Clark College, Atlanta University, and
Southern University, to which no visits had been made
in 1960, received in 1970, 350,510, and 600 corporate
representatives, respectively. Now Willie may not be
impressed with these figures, but I must confess that I
am. The vigorous recruitment of highly educated
blacks by corporations is one of the principal reasons
why the proportion of black male workers in white-
collar positions increased from 16 to 24 percent from
1964 to 1974 (the proportion of white males in white-
collar positions remained slightly over 40 percent during this period) with the greater portion of this increase
occurring in the higher level technical, professional,
and administrative positions. Indeed, as David Whitman has observed, in the 1960s "the number of blacks
in professional and technical positions increased by 131
percent while the number of blacks in managerial and
administrative positions increased by 67 percent."
Willie, however, chooses to ignore these unprecedented
gains for highly trained and educated blacks, preferr-
ing instead to emphasize the frustrations of black
violinist in the New York Philharmonic and to belittle
my statement that "talented and educated blacks are
now entering positions of prestige and influence at a
rate comparable to or, in some situations, exceeding
that of whites with equivalent qualifications."

However, despite the fact that younger educated
black males have finally reached income parity with
younger educated white males, and despite the rapid
increase in the number of blacks in higher paying
white-collar positions, there is still a significant income
gap between all college educated whites and all college
educated blacks because of the substantially lower in-

come of older educated blacks. But is this mainly a consequence of present-day discrimination as Willie wants to believe? No, the comparatively low incomes of older educated blacks is one of the legacies of past discrimination. Denied the opportunity to move into the higher paying occupations when they graduated from college or discouraged from even pursuing such occupational careers, older black college graduates tended to be concentrated in the lower paying fields such as teaching, social welfare, and segregated services; rarely were they employed as managers and professionals in large corporations upon entering the labor market. They therefore, in the words of Freeman, "lack the relevant training or managerial experience to take advantage of new opportunities and advanced only modedrately in the new job market." Nonetheless younger educated blacks are now entering, and indeed are encouraged to enter, previously neglected fields such as finance, management, chemistry, engineering, accounting, and computer science. Clifton B. Wharton, Jr., Chancellor of the State University of New York, points out, for example, that "in 1966, 45 percent of all Black undergraduates were majoring in education; today only 26 percent are. In 1966 only 5 percent of the Blacks were studying business, today 18 percent are." For all these reasons and despite modest gains in recent years, the income of older educated black males lags significantly behind the income of older educated white males. For all these reasons younger college educated black males have reached income parity with younger college educated white males.

COLLEGE EDUCATED BLACK WOMEN

Finally, I should say something about college educated women, another important subgroup hidden in Willie's statistics. College-trained black women like college-trained white women have been victimized by sex discrimination over the years. Indeed in the 1970s the major job market problems confronting female black college graduates are associated with sexual and not racial differences. By 1973, for example, although their earnings were significantly below those of both black and white male college graduates, female black college graduates earned nearly $1,000 more than their white counterparts.

BASIC ECONOMIC CHANGES

But I have yet to say anything about less privileged blacks. A comparison of their situation with the unprecedented gains of educated blacks demonstrates, in very sharp relief, the growing class divisions in the black community and the inadequacy of conventional explanations of racial experience. In interpreting my discussion about the improved job situation for more privileged blacks, Willie manages to infer that I "projected these findings upon the poor" because of my statement that "in view of these *developments* (my emphasis) it would be difficult to argue that the plight of the underclass is solely a consequence of racial oppression, that is, the explicit and overt efforts to keep blacks subjugated...." However, the developments to which I refer and which are discussed in several preceding sentences on the same page, are mainly concerned with the creation of a segmented labor market that has grown out of recent structural shifts in our economy--a labor market providing greatly different mobility opportunities for different segments of the black population. This is one of the central arguments of my book, an argument which reflects my concern about the effects of basic economic changes in advanced industrial society, an argument that Willie curiously ignores while he strains to place "the individual mobility" tag on my approach. The consequences of ignoring these structural dimensions in explaining inequality, as far as the black poor are concerned, is one of the subjects to which I now turn.

BLACK UNDERCLASS

When I argue that "the black experience has moved historically from economic racial oppression experienced by virtually all blacks to economic subordination for the black underclass," Willie complains that I cancel "out racial discrimination as a key cause of poverty among blacks" thereby making it difficult to explain the greater proportion of black families in poverty and the higher unemployment rate for younger blacks. Once again Willie overlooks or chooses to ignore one of my key arguments, namely that "one of the legacies of the racial oppression in previous years is the continued disproportionate black representation in the underclass." In other words, patterns of racial subjugation in the past created a vast black underclass as the accumulation of disadvantages were passed on from generation to generation, and the economic and technological revolution of modern industrial society threatens to insure it a permanent status. Accordingly, even if all racial discrimination were eliminated today, the situation of poor blacks will not be substantially improved unless something is done to remove the structural barriers to decent jobs created by changes in our system of production.

Thus, while Willie and some other social scientists continue to stess the problems of race at the expense of emphasizing the problems of economic dislocation under advanced capitalism, class divisions related to greatly different mobility opportunities are growing more rapidly in the black community than in the white community. For example, while young black male college graduates have reached income parity with comparable whites, the income of young black male high school graduates continues to lag behind the income of young white high school graduates. Whereas government antidiscrimination programs, such as affirmative action, have helped to enhance the economic opportunities of trained and educated blacks, such programs have not noticeable improved the economic conditions of poor blacks.

Unlike the life experiences of young privileged blacks, the growing number of black teenagers and young adults who are isolated in ghettoes and are crippled in inferior inner-city schools do not have the same access to higher paying jobs for which they are qualified as do young whites with similar levels of formal education. Because of the lack of job expansion in the manufacturing sector and the fact that desirable jobs in the service industries require education and training, it matters little whether or not poor blacks graduate from ghetto high schools when they face a situation in which the better paid and more desirable jobs which they can obtain without special skills and/or higher education are decreasing in central cities, not only in relative terms but sometimes in absolute numbers.

In short, because of the historical consequences of racial oppression, underclass blacks find themselves in a situation where they are particularly vulnerable to the negative consequences of uneven economic growth, increasing technology and automation, industry relocation, and labor market segmentation. These are difficult problems that are not going to be addressed by programs based simply upon the premise that current racial discrimination is the major cause of poor blacks' present miseries and limited life chances. Rather these are problems that define the conditions of class subordination, problems that grew out of the previous conditions of racial subordination and are now exacerbated by the economic changes of advanced industrial society. But to repeat, not all blacks are experiencing these difficulties. I would like to make just one more but very important point, in this regard--namely, the growing influence of class background on black experiences with both higher and lower education.

CLASS AND BLACK EDUCATION

According to Willie, the opposition from white professionals to minority admission policies in colleges and universities indicates "that talented and educated blacks are not being given access to privilege and power" at a rate comparable to that of whites with equivalent qualifications. Fortunately, this conclusion is not supported by recent data on school enrollment from the U.S. Bureau of the Census. The number of blacks attending colleges and universities in the United States increased from 340,000 in 1966 to 948,000 in 1975. Wharton points out that today the figure has increased to more than a million. Describing the figures on growing black college enrollments as "awesome," he states that "Blacks, who make up 11 percent of America's population, now make up to 10 percent of the 10.6 million college students...In one year, 1974, the percentage of Black high school graduates actually exceeded the percentage of White high school graduates going to college." And whereas almost half of all black college students were enrolled in predominantly Negro colleges in 1966, today almost 80 percent are attending predominantly white institutions. "These young people constitute the largest concentration of Black intellectual manpower in the entire world," states Wharton, "there is now a higher percentage of Blacks going to college in America than there is whites going to college in almost every European nation."

It goes without saying that this rapid rise in black college attendance has enormous implications for the further growth of the black middle class. The class stratification that we observed in the black community today may only be a vague outline of what is to come. This is particularly true when we consider that class or family background for blacks, as shown in the research of the economist Richard B. Freeman and the sociologists Robert Hauser and David Featherman, is becoming an increasingly important factor in determining overall educational attainment and who goes to college. In this connection Freeman points out that "despite all the attention given to enrollment of the ghetto poor into college, it was the children of better educated and wealthier parents who went in increasing numbers in the 1960s." More recent data from the U.S. Department of Commerce reinforce Freeman's conclusion. For example, only 17 percent of both black and white families with incomes of less than $5,000 a year had at least one member (age 18-24) attending college in 1974, and the percentage of family members enrolled in college tended to increase for both blacks and whites as family income increased. Families with incomes of $15,000 had the highest proportion of young adults in college (42 percent for blacks and 50 percent for whites).

But we do not have to restrict ourselves to the examination of the facts on higher education to see the significance of class background in black education and the gap between the haves and the have-nots in the black community. An even more revealing picture emerges when we juxtapose the figures on black higher education with those on black lower education. Specifically, while nearly an equal percentage of white and black high school graduates are entering college, the percentage of young blacks graduating from high school lags significantly behind the percentage of white high school graduates. In 1974, 85 percent of young white adults (20 to 24 years old) but only 72 percent of young black adults graduated from high school. Moreover, only 68 percent of young black adult males graduated from high school. And of those young blacks (18 to 24 years old) who were not enrolled in college and whose family income was less than $5,000, a startling 46 percent did not graduate from high school (the comparable white figure was 39 percent).

Thus, as the class divisions of the black community grow, it will become increasingly difficult for Willie and other social scientists to mask these differences either by speaking of a uniform or single black experience or by presenting gross statistics that neither reflect significant variations in the resources of various subgroups within the black population nor the differences in the effects of race in the past and the effects of race in the present. Andrew Brimmer's warning in 1969 that there is a deepening economic schism in the black community is clearly revealed in the black income, occupational, and educational differences discussed above. And they underscore the central argument of *The Declining Significance of Race* that class has become more important than race in determining black life chances.

WILLIE'S COUNTERHYPOTHESIS

Willie concludes his article by proclaiming that the significance of race is increasing, especially for middle-class blacks who are encountering whites for the first time in integrated situations, for example, in racially integrated neighborhoods. He therefore feels that the "people who most experience the pain of dislocation due to the changing times are the racial minorities who are talented and educated and integrated, not those who are impoverished and isolated." After resisting my arguments concerning the growing class differences in the black community, Willie circuitously acknowledges the progress of talented and educated blacks by discussing the psychological discomforts and pains of dislocation that have accompanied their movement into integrated situations.

Let me say, first of all, that when I speak of the declining significance of race, I am referring to the role it now plays in determining black life chances—in other words, the changing impact of race in the economic sector and, in particular, the importance of race in changing mobility opportunities. Thus, as I have tried to show, as the barriers to entering mainstream occupations were removed for educated blacks, they began to move away from the lower paying professions such as teaching and social work and began in significant numbers to prepare themselves for careers in finance, management, chemistry, engineering, accounting, and other professional areas. Nowhere in my book do I argue that race is "irrelevant or insignificant." It is not simply an either-or situation, rather it is a matter of degree. And I strongly emphasized that there is still a strong basis for racial antagonism on the social, community, and political level.

I do not disagree with the way in which Willie has proposed his counterhypothesis. Many educated blacks do experience psychological discomfort in new integrated situations. Willie and I could probably draw many personal examples of this. We both are black, and we both teach at elite universities. A few years ago almost no blacks were in such positions. But I am sure that neither of us would trade places with a poor black trapped in the ghetto and handcuffed to a menial, dead-end, and poorly paid job. That is the real problem in the black community, and no cries about the psychological discomfort of the integrated black elite should distract our attention from the abominable and deleterious physical conditions of the isolated black poor.

READINGS SUGGESTED BY THE AUTHOR

Featherman, David L. and Hauser, Robert M. "Changes in the Socioeconomic Stratification of the Races, 1962-73." *American Journal of Sociology* 82 (November 1976): 621-649.

Freeman, Richard B. *Black Elite: The New Market for Highly Educated Black Americans.* New York: McGraw-Hill, 1976.

Wharton, Jr., Clifton R. "Education and Black Americans: Yesterday, Today and Tomorrow." Paper presented at the New York State Black and Puerto Rican Legislative Caucus, Inc., and New York State Conference of Branches, NAACP, February 19, 1978.

Whitman, David. "The Changing Nature of Race Relations since the *Civil Rights Act,*" Unpublished manuscript. Amherst College, Amherst Massachusetts, April 1978.

Wilson, William Julius. *The Declining Significance of Race: Black and Changing American Institutions.* Chicago: University of Chicago Press, 1978.

STATEMENT OF THE ASSOCIATION OF BLACK SOCIOLOGISTS

The Association of Black Sociologists is concerned that the book by Professor William Julius Wilson entitled *The Declining Significance of Race* was considered sufficiently factual to merit the Spivack award from the American Sociological Association.

The book clearly omits significant data regarding the continuing discrimination against blacks at all class levels. It misinterprets even facts presented in the volume, and draws inferences that are contrary to the conclusions that other black and white scholars have reached with reference to the salience of race as a critical variable in American society.

It is the consensus of this organization that this book denies the overwhelming evidence regarding the significance of race and the literature that speaks to the contrary.

We certainly do not deny the freedom of any scholar to publish his or her work. However, it is the position of this organization that the sudden national attention given to Professor Wilson's book obscures the problem of the persistent oppression of blacks. There is an abundance of evidence that documents the significance of race as a critical variable in the denial of opportunities for blacks. For example, the United States Department of Housing and Urban Development has recently published a study which systematically and carefully documents that blacks of all social classes experience pervasive discrimination. Even within the discipline of sociology discrimination has been rampant. In the seventy-three year history of the American Sociological Association only one black person has been elected president, and that was more than three decades ago.

In the past reactionary groups have seized upon inappropriate analyses as a basis for the further suppression of blacks. We would hope that this is not the intent of the recent recognition that has been given to Professor Wilson's book. It must be underscored that the life chances of blacks (e.g., employment, housing, health care, education, etc.) are shocking and that discrimination in some areas is so pervasive that the income and employment gaps between blacks and whites have widened.

The Association of Black Sociologists is outraged over the misrepresentation of the black experience. We are also extremely disturbed over the policy implications that may derive from this work and that, given the nature of American society, are likely to set in motion equally objectionable trends in funding, research and training.

September 6, 1978
For further information contact:

Wilbur Watson
Association of Black Sociologists
Morgan State University
Baltimore, Maryland

Index